AMERICAN WOMEN ACHIEVERS
HIGH-INTEREST NONFICTION

BY KATHRYN WHEELER

CARSON-DELLOSA PUBLISHING COMPANY, INC. • GREENSBORO, NORTH CAROLINA

CREDITS

Editor: Carrie Fox

Layout Design: Lori Jackson

Inside Illustrations: Nick Greenwood

Cover Design: Peggy Jackson and Nick Greenwood

Cover Illustration: Tara Tavonatti

This book has been correlated to state, national, and Canadian provincial standards. Visit *www.carsondellosa.com* to search for and view its correlations to your standards.

© 2008, Carson-Dellosa Publishing Company, Inc., Greensboro, North Carolina 27425. The purchase of this material entitles the buyer to reproduce worksheets and activities for classroom use only—not for commercial resale. Reproduction of these materials for an entire school or district is prohibited. No part of this book may be reproduced (except as noted above), stored in a retrieval system, or transmitted in any form or by any means (mechanically, electronically, recording, etc.) without the prior written consent of Carson-Dellosa Publishing Co., Inc.

Printed in the USA • All rights reserved. ISBN 978-1-60022-969-5

AMERICAN WOMEN ACHIEVERS
TABLE OF CONTENTS

Introduction 4

Abigail Adams (1744–1818) 5

Phillis Wheatley (1753?–1784) 8

Sacagawea (1788?–1812?) 11

Maria Mitchell (1818–1889) 14

Harriet Tubman (1819?–1913) 17

Susan B. Anthony (1820–1906) 20

Emily Dickinson (1830–1886) 23

Mary Edwards Walker (1832–1919) 26

Louisa May Alcott (1832–1888) 29

Queen Liliuokalani (1838–1917) 32

Mary Cassatt (1844–1926) 35

Juliette "Daisy" Gordon Low (1860–1927) 38

Mary McLeod Bethune (1875–1955) 41

Helen Keller (1880–1968) 44

Jeannette Rankin (1880–1973) 47

Eleanor Roosevelt (1884–1962) 50

Mary Pickford (1892–1979) 53

Amelia Earhart (1897–1937) 56

Margaret Bourke-White (1904–1971) 59

Rachel Carson (1907–1964) 62

Virginia Apgar (1909–1974) 65

Babe Didrikson Zaharias (1911–1956) 68

Rosa Parks (1913–2005) 71

Eunice Shriver (1921– ____) 74

Maria Tallchief (1925– ____) 77

Althea Gibson (1927–2003) 80

Sandra Day O'Connor (1930– ____) 83

Toni Morrison (1931– ____) 86

Rita Moreno (1931– ____) 89

Madeleine Albright (1937– ____) 92

Pat Mora (1942– ____) 95

Isabel Allende (1942– ____) 98

Antonia Novello (1944– ____) 101

Sue Hendrickson (1949– ____) 104

Sally Ride (1951– ____) 107

Oprah Winfrey (1954– ____) 110

Nancy Lopez (1957– ____) 113

Ellen Ochoa (1958– ____) 116

Maya Lin (1959– ____) 119

Sarah Chang (1980– ____) 122

Answer Key 125

Assessment Grid 128

INTRODUCTION

Invite students to experience the thrill of reading with the historical biographies in *American Women Achievers: High-Interest Nonfiction*.

The passages in this book are appropriate for students in the intermediate grades. Among these grade levels, and even within individual classrooms, you will find learners at different reading levels. When presenting students with a new text, there is always the danger of frustrating struggling readers or boring students who have jumped ahead. To help all of these students maintain interest and find success in their reading assignments, this book presents each passage at two different reading levels.

Also included with each passage are a set of comprehension questions that applies to both versions of the story and a bonus activity. The questions test students' skills in determining main ideas, using context clues, sequencing, reading for details, and drawing conclusions. The assessment grid at the back of the book makes it easy to see which reading comprehension skills each student has mastered.

Each bonus activity is a writing extension that reinforces reasoning skills and encourages students to connect prior knowledge with the text.

An icon in the lower right or left corner of each passage page designates the reading level.

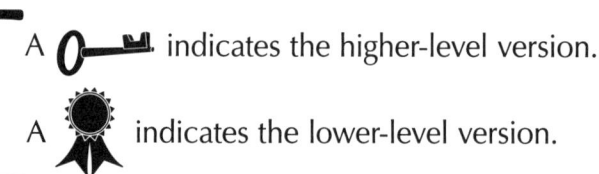

A 🗝 indicates the higher-level version.

A 🏅 indicates the lower-level version.

Use the rubric below to help you assess students' writing after they complete the bonus activity following each passage.

	NOVICE	EMERGING	INDEPENDENT	DISTINGUISHED
TOPIC	Did not stay on topic	Stayed on topic for most of the paragraph	Stayed on topic	Stayed on topic with elaboration
ORGANIZATION	Not organized	Organized	Well organized	Outstanding organization
WRITTEN EXPRESSION	Hard to understand	Easier to understand	Easy to understand	Well written, elaborated

ABIGAIL ADAMS
(1744–1818)

When John Adams met Abigail Smith, she was 15 years old. She was smart, witty, and loved to read. John later said that he had made up his mind almost at once that he would marry Abigail. She was not like anyone else he knew.

John Adams was right. Abigail was very different from most women of her time. And, her ideas and advice would become a part of American history.

In the 1700s, most women were guided by their husbands. Abigail was not. She had strong ideas of her own. She and John wrote each other more than 1,000 letters during their lives. In her letters, Abigail spoke her mind. In one letter, she asked John to put into the Declaration of Independence that women were free, just as men were. This was not an idea that most people had at the time. But, Abigail was different.

Abigail was against slavery. One time, a servant boy asked for her help so that he could learn to read and write. Abigail had taught all of her own children. She taught this boy, too. Then, she helped him get into a school. When a neighbor told her that it was wrong to help black people learn to read, Abigail said that the boy was free and she had been proud to help him.

At that time, it was against the law for women to own land. Abigail wanted her husband to change that law. She knew that women could run farms, because she did it herself. John was gone most of the time. Abigail chose the crops, bought and sold land, and bought farm animals. She was so good at this important job that the Adams family grew rich.

In the 1780s, John needed to travel to France and England. He needed to form friendships for the new country of America. He also needed to get **loans** so that the country could grow. Abigail sailed to Europe to meet him there. She helped him through tricky meetings and talks. Later, John Adams became vice president, then was elected president in 1797. Abigail was by his side, helping him and speaking her mind, just as she always had. She was the first woman to live in the White House.

Abigail Adams was the first woman to be both the wife and the mother of presidents of the United States. Her son, John Quincy Adams, became president in 1824. But, Abigail holds her own place in history. There was nobody else like her, as John Adams knew from the start.

ABIGAIL ADAMS
(1744–1818)

John Adams met Abigail Smith when she was 15 years old. She was smart and funny. She loved to read. John said later that he had known right away that he would marry Abigail. She was not like anyone else he knew.

John Adams was right. Abigail was very different from most women of her time. Her ideas became a part of history.

Most women at the time were guided by their husbands. Abigail was not. She had strong ideas of her own. She and John wrote each other more than 1,000 letters. Abigail spoke her mind in all of them. In one letter, she told John that women were free, just like men. She wanted him to add that to the Declaration of Independence. It was not an idea that most people had at the time. But, Abigail was different.

Abigail thought that it was wrong to own slaves. One time, a servant boy asked for her help. He wanted to read and write. Abigail had taught all of her own children. She taught this boy, too. Then, she helped him get into a school. A neighbor told her that it was wrong to help black people learn to read. Abigail said that the boy was free and she had been proud to help him.

At that time, it was against the law for women to own land. Abigail wanted her husband to change that law. She knew that women could run farms. She ran a farm herself. John was gone most of the time. Abigail chose the crops. She bought and sold land. She bought farm animals. She was very good at her job. The Adams family grew rich.

John had to go to France and England in the 1780s. He needed to find friends for the new country of America. He needed **loans** so that the country could grow. Abigail joined him there. She helped him through tricky meetings and talks. Later, John Adams became vice president. Then, he became president in 1797. Abigail was by his side. She helped him. She spoke her mind, just as she always had.

Abigail Adams was the first woman to live in the White House. She was married to one president. She was the mother of another. Her son, John Quincy Adams, became president in 1824. But, Abigail has her own place in history. There was nobody else like her.

American Women Achievers • CD-104255 • © Carson-Dellosa

NAME: _____ DATE: _____

ABIGAIL ADAMS
(1744–1818)

1. Choose a good title for this story.
   a. First Lady in the White House
   b. John Quincy Adams's Mother
   c. The Amazing Life of Abigail Adams
   d. The Woman Who Was Different

2. What does the word **loans** mean in the passage?
   a. gifts of money
   b. money that is borrowed and later paid back
   c. makes a gift of something of value
   d. sells something for money

3. Number the following events in the order they happened.
   _____ Abigail Adams ran the family farm.
   _____ Abigail went to England and France to help her husband.
   _____ Abigail Smith married John Adams.
   _____ Abigail's son became president of the United States.
   _____ Abigail Adams became First Lady.

4. Answer the following questions.
   What did Abigail want added to the Declaration of Independence?
   _____
   _____

   How did Abigail Adams feel about slavery?
   _____
   _____

   Why was Abigail so sure that women could own land and run farms?
   _____
   _____
   _____

   Who was John Quincy Adams?
   _____
   _____

5. What does it mean to speak your mind?
   a. to say what you think
   b. to say everything that you're thinking all at once
   c. to think about your ideas, but not say them
   d. to listen to and respect something that someone else says

---

BONUS

Do you write letters or e-mails to family members or friends? Write a letter that tells how you feel about a current event or something you saw on the news.

© Carson-Dellosa • CD-104255 • American Women Achievers

PHILLIS WHEATLEY
(1753?–1784)

The young girl sat at her own desk. She **gazed** out the window, then started to write. She was working on a poem. This was an amazing scene in the 1700s. Why? This young girl was a slave.

Phillis Wheatley was stolen from her family in Africa. She was brought to Boston, Massachusetts, on a ship called *Phillis*. A kind woman named Susanna Wheatley saw the shivering little girl in the market. She bought her and named her after the ship that carried her to the New World.

Phillis was not treated like most slaves. She did not have to toil over housework. Instead, Mrs. Wheatley asked her own daughter to teach English to Phillis. Phillis learned to read and write quickly. Then, just as quickly, she learned Latin and Greek. Mrs. Wheatley discovered that Phillis started to compose poems. So, she gave Phillis plenty of time and a place to write. In these ways, Phillis was treated like the other children in the Wheatley family.

One day, a newspaper in Boston published one of Phillis's poems. Phillis explained to Mrs. Wheatley that she had written many poems, not just that one. Mrs. Wheatley wrote to a friend in London, England, who said that he would help Phillis get a book printed. Mrs. Wheatley even paid for Phillis to travel to London. She attended parties. She met Benjamin Franklin. Everyone talked about Phillis's beautiful poems. She amazed people with her knowledge and her talent.

But one day, Phillis received bad news. Mrs. Wheatley was ill. Phillis sailed on a ship back to Boston. Sadly, Mrs. Wheatley did not recover. She gave Phillis her freedom before she died.

Did Phillis ever write more poems? There are clues that she wrote another book, but it has vanished. We will probably never know what else Phillis had to say in her work. But even so, she has a place in history. Phillis Wheatley was the first female writer who was helped by other women to write and sell a book. The fact that she was an African American slave made this even more important.

PHILLIS WHEATLEY
(1753?–1784)

The young girl sat at her own desk. She **gazed** out the window. Then, she started to write. She was working on a poem. This was an amazing scene in the 1700s. Why? This young girl was a slave.

Phillis Wheatley was stolen from her family in Africa. She was brought to Boston, Massachusetts, on a ship called *Phillis*. A kind woman named Susanna Wheatley saw the little girl in the market. She bought her and named her Phillis, like the ship that carried her to the New World.

Phillis was not treated like most slaves. She did not have to do hard work in the home. Mrs. Wheatley asked her own daughter to teach English to Phillis. Phillis learned to read and write quickly. Then, she learned Latin and Greek. Mrs. Wheatley found out that Phillis started to write poems. So, she gave her a place and time to write. Phillis was treated like the other children in the Wheatley family.

One day, a newspaper in Boston printed one of Phillis's poems. Phillis told Mrs. Wheatley that she had written many more. Mrs. Wheatley wrote to a friend in London, England. He said that he would help Phillis get a book printed. Mrs. Wheatley even paid for Phillis to go to London. Phillis went to parties. She met Benjamin Franklin. Everyone talked about Phillis's beautiful poems. She amazed people with her knowledge and her talent.

But one day, Phillis got bad news. Mrs. Wheatley was ill. Phillis sailed on a ship back to Boston. Mrs. Wheatley did not get better. She gave Phillis her freedom before she died.

Did Phillis ever write more poems? There are clues that she wrote another book. But, that book has been lost. We may never know what else Phillis had to say. But, she has a place in history. Phillis Wheatley was the first female writer who was helped by other women to write and sell a book. The fact that she was a slave made this even more important.

NAME: _____   DATE: _____

PHILLIS WHEATLEY
(1753?–1784)

1. This story is mainly about:

   a. the first female poet who was helped by men.

   b. a young woman who went across the ocean.

   c. a slave whose life was like that of many other slaves.

   d. a slave who wrote poems, was treated kindly, and was later freed.

2. What does the word **gazed** mean in the passage?

   a. thought hard

   b. stared

   c. covered with frosting

   d. wrote something

3. Number the following events in the order they happened.

   _____ Phillis Wheatley was sold in a market in Boston, Massachusetts.

   _____ A newspaper printed one of Phillis's poems.

   _____ Phillis learned to read and write.

   _____ Mrs. Wheatley died.

   _____ Phillis wrote her first book of poems.

4. Answer the following questions.

   How did Susanna Wheatley help Phillis get her book printed?
   _____
   _____

   What details in the story show that Phillis was treated well?
   _____
   _____
   _____

   Which famous person did Phillis meet in London, England?
   _____

   Why did Phillis come home from London?
   _____
   _____

5. What happened to Phillis's second book of poems?

   a. It was also printed in London.

   b. It was hidden and Phillis could not find it again.

   c. Phillis did not like the new poems, so she threw the book away.

   d. Nobody knows what happened to the second book of poems.

BONUS

Write a poem about your childhood. What do you remember best?

---

10   American Women Achievers • CD-104255 • © Carson-Dellosa

SACAGAWEA
(1788?–1812?)

The Hidatsa tribe watched closely as a group of white men set up an elaborate winter camp. Who were these strangers? What did they want? At first, no one knew that this group was unlike other groups of white men that they encountered in the past. The men were not fur traders but a group with a different job to do. They were explorers. The men were being led west by Meriwether Lewis and William Clark on an expedition to map new land recently bought by the United States. The year was 1804.

One girl in the Hidatsa tribe, who was only 16 years old, knew what it felt like to be a stranger. Her name was Sacagawea, and she was from the Shoshone tribe. But during a raid by the Hidatsa tribe, she was taken from her family and brought east, far from her home. Then, she married a French trader. Together, she and her husband lived in the Hidatsa village. That winter, she gave birth to their first child.

Lewis and Clark heard that Sacagawea grew up somewhere in the West. The explorers wanted her help because she knew the country where they were headed. She knew the languages of other tribes and could help the men trade for the horses they needed to ride over the mountains. Lewis and Clark offered the young woman a job.

Sacagawea and her husband left with the group the next May. The young American Indian helped the explorers in a variety of ways. Because of her, the tribes that the group encountered knew right away that the travelers came in peace. How? Sacagawea and her son were with them. No war party would travel with a woman and a baby.

As the group went west, Sacagawea started to see **landmarks** she knew. She was able to forage for food for the group. She even remembered the easiest path through the northern Rocky Mountains.

Then, something amazing happened. The group needed horses and came to a village. The chief of the tribe turned out to be Sacagawea's brother! Sacagawea walked up to him and pulled her blanket around him, the sign that they were from the same family. The chief was overjoyed to see his lost sister again.

There was a feast and dancing that night, but soon it was time for the group to go on their way. Sacagawea could have chosen to stay with her family and her tribe. Instead, she headed west with Lewis and Clark. She wanted to ride over the mountains and go all the way to the ocean. This young mother discovered that she had the heart of a true explorer.

SACAGAWEA
(1788?–1812?)

When the group of white men set up their winter camp, the Hidatsa tribe watched carefully. Who were these strangers? What did they want? At first, no one knew that these men were not fur traders like other white men whom the tribe had seen. This group had a new job to do. They were explorers. The men were being led west by Meriwether Lewis and William Clark. Their job was to map the new land bought by the United States. It was 1804.

One girl in the tribe, who was only 16 years old, knew what it felt like to be a stranger. Her name was Sacagawea. She was from the Shoshone tribe. But during a raid by the Hidatsa tribe, she had been taken east, far from her home. Then, she married a French trader. She and her husband lived in the Hidatsa village together. That winter, she had their first child.

Lewis and Clark heard that Sacagawea grew up somewhere in the West. They wanted her help. She knew the country. She knew the languages of other tribes. She could help the men trade for the horses that they would need to ride over the mountains. Lewis and Clark offered the young woman a job.

Sacagawea and her husband left with the group the next May. The young American Indian helped the explorers in many ways. Tribes knew right away that the travelers came in peace. How? They had Sacagawea and her son with them. No war party would travel with a woman and a baby.

As the group went west, Sacagawea started to see **landmarks** she knew. She was able to find food for the group. She even knew the easiest path through the northern Rocky Mountains.

Then, something amazing happened. The group needed horses. They came to a village. The chief of the tribe was Sacagawea's brother! Sacagawea walked up to him. She pulled her blanket around him. That was the sign that they were from the same family. The chief was overjoyed to see his lost sister again.

There was a feast and dancing that night. But, soon it was time for the group to go on their way. Sacagawea could have stayed with her family and her tribe. Instead, she went with Lewis and Clark. She wanted to ride over the mountains. She wanted to go all the way to the ocean. This young mother found that she had the heart of a true explorer.

12

American Women Achievers • CD-104255 • © Carson-Dellosa

NAME: _____ DATE: _____

SACAGAWEA
(1788?–1812?)

1. The sixth paragraph is mainly about:

    a. Sacagawea's childhood.

    b. Sacagawea's help to the explorers.

    c. how Sacagawea came to be hired by the explorers.

    d. how Sacagawea found her family again.

2. What does the word **landmarks** mean in the passage?

    a. markings on the ground that show where a road will be built

    b. maps

    c. familiar places or features

    d. events in history

3. Number the following events in the order they happened.

    _____ Sacagawea married a French trader.

    _____ Sacagawea traveled west with the explorers.

    _____ Sacagawea found her brother.

    _____ Sacagawea was taken from her family during a raid on her village.

    _____ Sacagawea gave birth to a baby.

4. Answer the following questions.

    Who were Lewis and Clark?

    _____

    _____

    What tribe took Sacagawea east?

    _____

    How did the explorers meet Sacagawea's tribe?

    _____

    _____

    How did Sacagawea help the explorers?

    _____

    _____

5. What was the reason for Lewis and Clark's trip west?

    a. They were trying to find a way across the Rocky Mountains.

    b. They were mapping the new land that was just bought by the United States.

    c. They were looking for gold and silver.

    d. They were buying horses for the United States government.

BONUS

Write a story from Sacagawea's point of view. Have her tell about one day that she spent with the explorers and what it was like to travel with them.

© Carson-Dellosa • CD-104255 • American Women Achievers

MARIA MITCHELL
(1818–1889)

Maria Mitchell was lucky. In a time when people thought that women did not need to learn, Maria's father thought that both boys and girls should go to school. Maria went to school, but she also learned at home. Her father was one of her main teachers. By the time she was 12 years old, Maria was her father's assistant as he studied the stars.

As an adult, Maria took a job at the library near her home. That way, she could work and still read and learn all day. At night, she and her father used his telescope to look at the sky.

In October 1847, Maria was looking at the sky. She saw a bright star through the telescope. She was sure that she had never seen it before. Maria wondered if it could be a **comet**. She carefully wrote down notes. The next night, it looked as if the "star" had moved! It had a tail! Now, Maria was sure that she had found a comet, not a star.

At that time, the king of Denmark was offering a prize to the first person who found a comet that could be seen only through a telescope. Maria won the prize. It was a gold medal. But, she won something else, too. She won people's respect, and they saw that she was serious about her work. The American Academy of Arts and Sciences voted her in as a member. She was the first female member of the Academy.

In 1865, a special school opened, a college just for women called Vassar College. Maria became a teacher, or professor, there. She was the first female professor to teach astronomy, the science of the stars and planets. Her students loved her because she believed that women could do important scientific work. In 1868, there was a huge meteor shower. Maria and her students mapped the paths of 4,000 of these "shooting stars." Her students also aided Maria as she made maps of the surfaces of Jupiter and Saturn.

In 1878, Maria took four of her students on a trip. They traveled more than 2,000 miles west so that they could study an eclipse of the sun. Maria and her students camped in tents. At that time, women did not travel far without men or go camping on their own. But, Maria did not care. What she cared about was teaching and learning about the night sky. Because of her influence, female students learned that they could be scientists. They could make valuable discoveries to help us understand our world.

MARIA MITCHELL
(1818–1889)

Maria Mitchell was born at a time when people thought that girls did not need to go to school. But, Maria was lucky. Her father did not think this. He thought that both boys and girls should learn. Maria went to school. She also learned at home. Her father was one of her main teachers. When she was 12 years old, Maria became his helper as he studied the stars.

When she got older, Maria took a job at the library near her home. That way, she could work and still read and learn all day. At night, she and her father used his telescope to look at the sky.

One night, Maria was looking at the sky. It was in October 1847. She saw a bright star through the telescope. She was sure that she had never seen it before. Could it be a **comet**? She carefully made notes. The next night, Maria looked again. The "star" had moved! It had a tail! Now, Maria was sure that she had found a comet, not a star.

The king of Denmark promised to give a prize to the first person who found a tiny comet with a telescope. It had to be a comet you could not see with just your eyes. Maria won the prize. It was a gold medal. But, she won something else, too. She won respect. People knew she was serious about her work. The American Academy of Arts and Sciences made her a member. She was the first woman in the Academy.

In 1865, a special school opened. It was a college for women. It was called Vassar College. Maria became a teacher, or professor, there. She was the first female professor to teach about the stars. Her students loved her. She believed that women could do important work in science. In 1868, there was a big shower of meteors. Maria and her students mapped the paths of 4,000 of these "shooting stars." Her students also helped Maria as she made maps of Jupiter and Saturn.

In 1878, Maria took four of her students on a trip. They went more than 2,000 miles west. Maria and her students camped in tents. They studied an eclipse of the sun. Women did not travel far without men at that time. They did not go camping on their own. But, Maria did not care. What she cared about was teaching and learning about the night sky. Because of her, female students learned that they could be scientists. They could make discoveries to help us understand our world.

NAME: _____ DATE: _____

MARIA MITCHELL
(1818–1889)

1. The first paragraph is mainly about:

   a. Maria Mitchell's first teaching job.
   b. Maria Mitchell's schooling.
   c. Maria Mitchell's trip west.
   d. Maria Mitchell's discovery.

2. What does the word **comet** mean in the passage?

   a. a body of ice with a "tail" of dust that orbits the sun
   b. a kind of planet
   c. a special type of star that moves very fast
   d. a kind of cleanser

3. Number the following events in the order they happened.

   _____ Maria Mitchell discovered a comet that could be seen only with a telescope.

   _____ Maria and her students made maps of meteor paths.

   _____ Maria Mitchell took her students on a trip to see an eclipse.

   _____ Maria Mitchell became her father's helper.

   _____ Maria was given a job as a college professor.

4. Answer the following questions.

   Who gave Maria Mitchell a gold medal?
   _____

   Why did Maria take a job at a library?
   _____
   _____
   _____

   What group made Maria its first female member?
   _____
   _____

   What was the name of the school where Maria taught?
   _____

5. Why do you think the author said that the medal won respect for Maria's work?

   a. Before her discovery of the comet, people might not have taken a female scientist seriously.
   b. Before she won a medal, Maria was not serious about her work studying the sky.
   c. Before the king of Denmark gave Maria a prize, she was ready to quit trying to be a scientist.
   d. Before Maria found the comet, nobody thought that people would ever see comets through telescopes.

BONUS

Stay up one night and watch the night sky. You can watch with your eyes or through a telescope. Take notes. Then, write a report about all of the things that you saw.

HARRIET TUBMAN
(1819?–1913)

The slave woman looked up in the sky at the North Star. She found her way carefully from one friendly house to another. In this way, Harriet Tubman escaped using the Underground Railroad. It was a secret system of safe houses and helpful people. They helped slaves get to freedom. Harriet ran away to Philadelphia, Pennsylvania. She knew that she could live there as a free person.

Running away from slavery was difficult and dangerous. If a slave was caught, he was punished, then sent back to his life as a slave. But, Harriet was very brave. Once she was free, she wanted to help other people become free, too. She could have stayed where she was safe, in her new home in Philadelphia. Instead, she returned to the South.

First, she helped her sister, her nieces, and her nephews escape from slavery. Then, she went back to help other slaves.

Harriet worked this way for 10 years, from 1850 to 1860. She guided 300 slaves to the North and freedom. Then, the Civil War broke out. But, Harriet was not going to stop helping people. She chose to do something that was even more dangerous than her Underground Railroad work.

Harriet worked as a spy. Many women worked as spies during the war. But, few of them took as many **risks** as Harriet did. Because she was black, she was in danger of being sent back to slavery or even being killed. But, Harriet knew the land in the South. She knew how to travel secretly, without being caught. She spied on soldiers at their camps. She found out things that helped the army of the North.

Harriet even led a group of black soldiers on a raid, during which the group freed more than 700 slaves. No other woman had ever led American soldiers on a raid before. Nothing could stop Harriet from helping people who needed her.

When she was not spying, Harriet worked as a nurse. She helped take care of African American soldiers and slaves who had been wounded. After the war, Harriet helped the freed slaves. She opened a home to take care of old people. She worked for the rights of women. Harriet Tubman was one of the strongest and bravest women in American history.

HARRIET TUBMAN
(1819?–1913)

The slave woman looked up in the sky at the North Star. She found her way from one friendly house to another. Harriet Tubman was running away. She used the Underground Railroad for help. It was a secret system of safe houses and people. They helped slaves get to freedom. Harriet went to Philadelphia, Pennsylvania. She knew that she could live there as a free person.

Running away from slavery was hard. It was filled with danger. If a slave was caught, he was punished and sent back to slavery. But, Harriet was very brave. Once she was free, she wanted to help other people become free, too. She could have stayed where she was safe. Instead, she went back to the South.

First, she helped her sister, her nieces, and her nephews run away. Then, she went back to help other slaves. She worked on the Underground Railroad.

Harriet worked this way for 10 years. She helped slaves run away from 1850 to 1860. Then, the Civil War started. But, Harriet was not going to stop helping people. She chose new work. It was filled with even more danger.

Harriet worked as a spy. Many women worked as spies during the war. But, few of them took as many **risks** as Harriet did. Because she was black, she was in danger of being caught. She could be sent back to being a slave or even be put to death. But, Harriet knew the land in the South. She knew ways to travel without being caught. She watched soldiers. She found out things to help the army of the North.

Harriet even led a group of black soldiers on a raid. During the raid, the group set more than 700 slaves free. No other woman had ever led American soldiers on a raid before. Nothing could stop Harriet. She wanted to help people who needed her.

Harriet also worked as a nurse. She took care of black soldiers and slaves who had been hurt. After the war, Harriet helped the freed slaves. She opened a home to take care of old people. She worked for the rights of women. She was one of the strongest and bravest women in American history.

NAME: _____ DATE: _____

HARRIET TUBMAN
(1819?–1913)

1. What is the main idea of this story?

    a. Harriet Tubman was a strong woman.

    b. Harriet Tubman was a slave who ran away.

    c. Harriet Tubman was a strong woman who spent her life helping others.

    d. Harriet Tubman was in the army during the Civil War.

2. What does the word **risks** mean in the passage?

    a. chances that might cause harm or loss

    b. secret messages

    c. investments with money

    d. games with dice

3. Number the following events in the order they happened.

    _____ Harriet worked for women's rights.

    _____ Harriet escaped to freedom in the North.

    _____ Harriet worked as a spy.

    _____ Harriet went back to the South to help her sister run away.

    _____ Harriet's work in helping slaves escape ended when the war started.

4. Answer the following questions.

    What did Harriet do during the war that no other woman had ever done?

    _____

    _____

    How did Harriet find her way to freedom when she ran away?

    _____

    _____

    What two jobs did Harriet have during the Civil War?

    _____

    _____

    Name one thing that Harriet did after the Civil War.

    _____

    _____

5. What role did Harriet have in the Underground Railroad?

    a. She ran a "station," or a safe house where slaves could rest.

    b. She helped build a special train.

    c. She was a "conductor," or someone who led slaves to safety.

    d. She drew maps to help slaves run away.

BONUS

Write a story about a slave who was helped by the Underground Railroad.

© Carson-Dellosa • CD-104255 • American Women Achievers

SUSAN B. ANTHONY
(1820–1906)

When Susan B. Anthony was young, women did not have many rights. If a woman worked, the money she made was given to her husband. If a woman was wronged, she could not go to court to sue and right the wrong. There were few jobs that women were allowed to do. Susan wanted to change these things.

Susan grew up in a stern home, where she was not allowed to play or have toys. But, she was sent to school and given a good education. When Susan started school, she already knew how to read. She had taught herself when she was only three years old.

Before the Civil War, Susan spoke out against the wrongs of slavery. But, she also wanted to help women of all races. She met Elizabeth Cady Stanton, who felt the same way. The two friends started a magazine that discussed rights for women. The magazine printed articles about how women should be paid the same as men.

In 1860, New York passed new laws that allowed married women to own land. They could also run shops and businesses. They could keep the wages they made when they worked. These changes came about mainly because of Susan's and Elizabeth's hard work, articles, and speeches.

After the Civil War, African American men were given the right to vote. Susan said that women should have that right, too. She and Elizabeth started an organization to get voting rights for women. In 1872, people were voting for a new president. Susan marched with a group of women. They tried to cast their own votes in the election. For this attempt, Susan was arrested. In 1873, her case went to court. She was told to pay a **fine**. Susan refused. She told the judge that she would never pay a single dollar because the fine was not just.

Susan took many trips across the country, giving speeches and leading large meetings about women's rights. She and Elizabeth worked on a book about the history of women and their fight for voting rights.

Susan was very sad when Elizabeth died in 1902. By that time, Susan was ill, too. But, she kept fighting. In 1906, Susan gave a famous speech. She told the women who came to hear her that they must not fail to get the right to vote, that failure was "impossible." Not long afterward, Susan died. It took another 14 long years before women could vote in the United States. Susan's work and words played a crucial role in this important change for female citizens.

SUSAN B. ANTHONY
(1820–1906)

When Susan B. Anthony was young, women did not have many rights. If a woman worked, the money she made was given to her husband. If a woman was wronged, she could not go to court to get help. There were few jobs that women were allowed to do. Susan wanted to change these things.

Susan grew up in a stern home. She did not play or have toys. But, she was sent to school. Susan already knew how to read when she started school. She had taught herself when she was only three years old.

Before the Civil War, Susan spoke out against slavery. But, she also wanted to help women of all races. She met Elizabeth Cady Stanton, who felt the same way. The two friends started a magazine. It talked about rights for women. It said that women should be paid the same as men.

In 1860, New York passed new laws. These laws said that married women could own land. They could run shops. They could keep the money they made when they worked. These changes came about mainly because of Susan's and Elizabeth's hard work, writing, and speeches.

After the Civil War, black men were given the right to vote. Susan said that women should have that right, too. She and Elizabeth started a group to get voting rights for women. In 1872, people voted for a new president. Susan marched with a group of women. They tried to cast their own votes. Susan was arrested. In 1873, her case went to court. She was told to pay a **fine**. Susan said no. She told the judge that she would never pay a dollar because the fine was not fair.

Susan took many trips across the country. She gave speeches. She led big meetings about women's rights. She and Elizabeth worked on a book. It was about women and the right to vote.

Elizabeth died in 1902. Susan was very sad. By that time, Susan was ill, too. But, she kept fighting. In 1906, Susan gave a well-known speech. She told the women who came to hear her that they must not fail to get the right to vote. Not long after that, Susan died. It took another 14 long years before women could vote in the United States. Susan's work and words played a big part in this important change for women.

© Carson-Dellosa • CD-104255 • American Women Achievers

NAME: _____ DATE: _____

SUSAN B. ANTHONY
(1820–1906)

1. The second paragraph is mainly about:

    a. Susan's childhood.

    b. Susan's magazine.

    c. Susan's stand against slavery.

    d. Susan's work after the Civil War.

2. What does the word **fine** mean in the passage?

    a. excellent

    b. money you pay when you have done something wrong

    c. very thin and delicate

    d. a term spent in jail

3. Number the following events in the order they happened.

    _____ Susan started school.

    _____ Susan was arrested for trying to vote.

    _____ Susan learned how to read.

    _____ Susan made her last speech about voting rights.

    _____ Susan traveled across the country to make speeches.

4. Answer the following questions.

    Who was Elizabeth Cady Stanton?

    _____

    _____

    What was the book about that Susan and Elizabeth wrote?

    _____

    _____

    Name one right that women did not have when Susan was young.

    _____

    What state passed important new laws for women's rights?

    _____

5. What happened after the Civil War that started Susan's fight for voting rights?

    a. Former slave women were told that they could vote.

    b. Susan was able to work on women's rights after the slaves were freed.

    c. Black men were given the right to vote, and Susan felt that women of all races should have that right, too.

    d. Susan met Abraham Lincoln, who told her to fight for voting rights for women.

BONUS

Read the first paragraph of the story again. Think about what it would be like in a world where men were allowed to do so many things that women were not. Choose one right women did not have. Write about why you think that everyone should have that right.

EMILY DICKINSON
(1830–1886)

The young woman was quiet and **shy**. Some people thought that she was strange. She hid in her room if her family had company. In writing to one person, she remarked that her best friends were the hills, the sunset, and "a dog large as myself."

This odd young woman was one of the greatest American poets of the 1800s. Her name was Emily Dickinson.

Emily lived in Amherst, a town in Massachusetts. Her grandfather had started a college there, and her father worked for the college. Emily was sent to good schools, but when she had to go away to college, she was so homesick that she came back in less than a year. After that, she stayed with her family. She did not like to meet strangers, so she spent a lot of time in her room. And during that time, Emily was always writing.

Emily's poems were very different from most poetry of the time. Her words were simple, not flowery. The lines of her poems ended in dashes, not commas or periods. She wrote about nature in a way that connected it to how people thought and felt. Even today, her poems seem modern.

During Emily's lifetime, few people knew that she wrote these poems. She rolled up many of them and locked them in her desk. She made little books of some of them, copying the poems and sewing the pages together with thread. During her life, about seven of her poems were published in newspapers. But after Emily died, her sister discovered that she had written almost 1,800 poems!

Emily might not have wanted her poems to be printed in books during her life. She might have found it hard for strangers to read her work. This was a young woman who baked gingerbread for children in her neighborhood but was too shy to hand it out to them. She would lower it to them in a basket from her bedroom window.

Even her best friend did not get to see Emily very often. Susan Gilbert married Emily's brother when Emily was 26. They lived next door to each other, but Emily would not walk outside to visit Susan. Instead, she wrote her letters almost every day.

After Emily died, her sister helped publish a book with some of her poems. Later, Emily's niece helped publish a book with more poems. Today, Emily is thought to be one of the most important American poets of the 1800s and one of the greatest female writers ever. Her quiet life led to work that will always be read and remembered.

EMILY DICKINSON
(1830–1886)

The young woman was quiet. She was **shy**. Some people thought that she was strange. She hid in her room if her family had company. She wrote to one person and said that her best friends were the hills, the sunset, and "a dog large as myself."

Her name was Emily Dickinson. She became one of the greatest poets of her time.

Emily lived in Amherst. That is a town in Massachusetts. Her grandfather had started a college there. Her father worked for the college. Emily was sent to good schools. She had to go away to college. But, Emily was so homesick that she came back in less than a year. After that, she stayed with her family. She did not like to meet strangers. She spent a lot of time in her room. And during that time, Emily was always writing.

Emily's poems were very different from most poetry of the time. Her words were simple, not flowery. The lines of her poems ended in dashes, not commas or periods. She wrote about nature. She connected it to how people thought and felt. Even today, her poems seem modern.

During Emily's life, few people knew that she wrote these poems. She rolled them up. She locked them in her desk. She made little books of some of them. She would copy the poems. Then, she would sew the pages together with thread. During her life, about seven of her poems were printed in newspapers. But after Emily died, her sister found that she had written almost 1,800 poems!

Emily might not have liked to see her poems in books during her life. She might not have liked strangers to read her work. This was a young woman who baked gingerbread for children in her neighborhood. But, she was too shy to give it to them. So, she would lower it to them in a basket from her bedroom window.

Even her best friend did not get to see Emily very often. Susan Gilbert married Emily's brother. Emily was 26 at the time. They lived next door to each other. But, Emily would not walk outside to visit Susan. Instead, she wrote her letters almost every day.

After Emily died, her sister helped make a book with some of her poems. Later, Emily's niece helped make a book with more poems. Today, Emily is thought to be one of the most important poets of the 1800s. People say that she was one of the greatest female writers ever. Her quiet life led to work that will always be read and remembered.

NAME: _____ DATE: _____

EMILY DICKINSON
(1830–1886)

1. What is the main idea of this story?

   a. Emily Dickinson did not like to leave her house.

   b. Emily Dickinson was a shy woman who became a great poet.

   c. Emily Dickinson locked herself in her room, and that is why she wrote so much.

   d. Emily Dickinson was a poet who was famous during her lifetime.

2. What does the word **shy** mean in the passage?

   a. timid

   b. wise

   c. little

   d. a and c

3. Number the following events in the order they happened.

   _____ Emily started college.

   _____ Emily's niece published a book of her aunt's poems.

   _____ Emily wrote letters to her best friend, Susan, after Susan married Emily's brother.

   _____ Emily Dickinson left college and came home for good.

   _____ Emily's sister found many of her poems after Emily died.

4. Answer the following questions.

   Where did Emily Dickinson live?
   _____

   Why didn't Emily finish college?
   _____
   _____

   What did Emily do with her poems after they were finished?
   _____
   _____

   Who was Susan?
   _____
   _____

5. Which of the following details shows Emily's shyness?

   a. She would not go outdoors to walk to her best friend's home.

   b. She would not go to the door to give her gingerbread to children.

   c. She would hide in her bedroom when her family had company.

   d. all of the above

BONUS

Watch a storm. Then, write a poem that describes the storm. Be sure to connect the storm to how you feel about it.

© Carson-Dellosa • CD-104255 • American Women Achievers

MARY EDWARDS WALKER
(1832–1919)

The soldiers could not believe their eyes. Their new doctor had arrived. The doctor wore a uniform just like the other men, but this was no man. Their doctor was a woman!

When Mary Edwards Walker finished medical school, she was the only woman in her class. She was only the second woman in the country to become a doctor. Now, these Civil War soldiers demanded that she be sent home. The head doctor remarked that she probably knew only as much about medicine as any common housewife.

But, Mary worked hard and saved lives. Some people even think that she worked as a spy for the North. While she was helping sick people in the South in April 1864, she got caught by Confederate soldiers. She was put into **prison** for four months. She was released when she was exchanged for a doctor from the South. By this time, the men in her unit knew that she was a good doctor, but the army would not let her work for pay until the very end of the war. She became the first female doctor in the United States Army in the fall of 1864.

At the end of the war in 1865, Mary was given the Medal of Honor. It was for her brave medical work on the battlefield. She remains the only woman who has ever been awarded this important honor.

After the war, Mary wrote books and gave speeches about women's rights. Mary was raised on a farm in New York. Her father thought that girls should dress the same as boys and should not have to wear tight corsets and big hoop skirts. Mary dressed like a man for much of her life. She gave speeches about the freedom of wearing comfortable clothing, like pants.

Mary also helped Susan B. Anthony fight for women's voting rights. Mary attempted to vote but was turned away at the polls. She wrote a letter pointing out that women were put in jail for not obeying the law but they did not have the right to vote on laws.

In 1890, before women could vote, Mary announced that she would run for Congress. In 1891, she ran for a seat in the Senate. She lost. Like many things in Mary's life, her run for Congress was a move ahead of its time.

In 1917, Congress took away Mary's Medal of Honor. She was told that only those who had fought in battles could have the honor. Mary would not give back the medal. She wore it every day until she died. In 1977, Mary's medal was restored by President Jimmy Carter. Today, you can see it on display at the Pentagon in Washington, D.C.

MARY EDWARDS WALKER
(1832–1919)

The soldiers could not believe their eyes. Their new doctor had come. The doctor wore a uniform, just like the other men. But, this was not a man. Their doctor was a woman!

When Mary Edwards Walker finished school, she was the only woman in her class. She was only the second woman in the country to become a doctor. Now, these Civil War soldiers asked that she be sent home. The head doctor said that she probably knew only as much about medicine as any housewife.

But, Mary worked hard. She saved lives. Some people think that she also worked as a spy for the North. She went to the South to help sick people in April 1864. She got caught. She was put into **prison** for four months. She got out when she was traded for a doctor from the South. By this time, the men in her unit knew that she was a good doctor. But, the army would not let her work for pay until the very end of the war. She became the first female doctor in the United States Army in the fall of 1864.

At the end of the war in 1865, Mary was given the Medal of Honor. It was for her brave work on the battlefield. She is still the only woman who has ever been given this important medal.

After the war, Mary wrote books. She gave speeches about women's rights. Mary was raised on a farm in New York. Her father thought that girls should dress the same as boys. They should not have to wear tight corsets and big hoop skirts. Mary dressed like a man for much of her life. She gave speeches about the freedom of wearing comfortable clothing, like pants.

Mary also helped Susan B. Anthony fight for the right to vote for women. Mary tried to vote. She was turned away. She wrote a letter. It pointed out that women were put in jail for not obeying the law but they did not have the right to vote on laws.

In 1890, before women could vote, Mary said that she would run for Congress. In 1891, she ran for a seat in the Senate. She lost. Like many things in Mary's life, her run for Congress was a move ahead of its time.

In 1917, Congress took away Mary's Medal of Honor. She was told that only those who had fought in battles could have the honor. Mary would not give back the medal. She wore it every day until she died. In 1977, Mary's medal was given back by President Jimmy Carter. Today, you can see it at the Pentagon in Washington, D.C.

NAME: _____   DATE: _____

MARY EDWARDS WALKER
(1832–1919)

1. What is the main idea of the last paragraph?

   a. Mary's Medal of Honor was taken away but later given back.

   b. Mary lost her Medal of Honor because she did not fight.

   c. Mary wore her Medal of Honor every day.

   d. Mary's Medal of Honor is at the Pentagon in Washington, D.C.

2. What does the word **prison** mean in the passage?

   a. to pry open

   b. a type of school

   c. a jail

   d. unit headquarters

3. Number the following events in the order they happened.

   _____ Mary was caught by soldiers from the South.

   _____ Mary was awarded the Medal of Honor.

   _____ Mary completed medical school.

   _____ Mary wrote books and gave speeches on women's rights.

   _____ Mary joined a unit of soldiers as their doctor.

4. Answer the following questions.

   Where was Mary Edwards Walker raised?
   _____

   How many female doctors were there in the United States before Mary became a doctor?
   _____

   Whom did Mary help fight for the right to vote?
   _____

   Who gave back Mary's Medal of Honor?
   _____

5. Why do you think Mary dressed like a man for most of her life?

   a. She liked the way pants looked.

   b. She did not own any hoop skirts and could not afford to buy them.

   c. She wanted to run for Congress.

   d. She wanted to wear comfortable clothes that would let her do her work.

BONUS

Write a paragraph stating why you think that it was right or wrong to give Mary Edwards Walker back her Medal of Honor.

American Women Achievers • CD-104255 • © Carson-Dellosa

LOUISA MAY ALCOTT
(1832–1888)

Louisa May Alcott is best known for her book *Little Women*. The book is based on her own family. Louisa had three sisters. One sister, like Meg in the book, was gentle and loved theater. One sister, like Amy, was an artist. And one sister, like Beth, died tragically when she was young. Was Louisa like Jo March, the tomboy and writer?

In some ways, she was. Louisa grew up in a poor family. Her father was a teacher, but many people did not like his theories about teaching. The family moved many times as her father moved from one job to the next. There was little money. Louisa was strong and independent. She loved to run races, climb trees, and write scary stories. Louisa felt from a young age that she must earn money so that she could help her family. She announced that she would do it by selling her writing.

In 1852, Louisa sold a poem. Then, in 1854, she sold her first book to a publisher. It was a start, but the book earned her only a small amount of money.

Then, the Civil War began, and Louisa went to Washington, D.C., in 1862. She worked as a nurse, taking care of soldiers. Then, she fell ill. She recovered, but Louisa had trouble for the rest of her life with complications from the illness.

Next, Louisa worked at a magazine for children. She was asked to write a book about girls. Louisa knew all about the lives of girls. After all, she grew up with three sisters! So, she wrote *Little Women*. The book was set during the Civil War.

Books for children in the 1860s were often **dull**, teaching lessons about how to be good and obedient. Louisa's book was different. The March sisters got into trouble, fought with each other, and made up. They went to parties and put on plays. They seemed real, and people loved reading about them.

After the book came out, Louisa earned enough money to help her family and pay their debts. She wrote more books about Jo March. She also wrote other stories that people loved.

Louisa bought a big house in Boston, Massachusetts, for her family. She kept writing until her death in 1888. By that time, Louisa was one of the best-loved writers in the country. Her books had sold a million copies. Today, people around the world still read Louisa's wonderful stories.

LOUISA MAY ALCOTT
(1832–1888)

Louisa May Alcott is best known for her book *Little Women*. The book is based on her own family. Louisa had three sisters. One sister, like Meg in the book, was gentle and loved theater. One sister, like Amy, was an artist. And one sister, like Beth, died young. Was Louisa like Jo March, the tomboy and writer?

In some ways, she was. Louisa grew up in a poor family. Her father was a teacher. But, many people did not like his ideas about teaching. The family moved many times as her father went from job to job. There was little money. Louisa was strong and tough. She loved to run races. She loved to climb trees. And, she loved to write scary stories. Louisa felt from a young age that she must earn money. She needed to help her family. She said that she would do it by selling her writing.

In 1852, Louisa sold a poem. Then, in 1854, she sold her first book. It was a start, but it earned her only a little bit of money.

Then, the Civil War began. Louisa went to Washington, D.C., in 1862. She worked as a nurse. She took care of soldiers. Then, she fell ill. She got better, but Louisa had trouble for the rest of her life from the illness.

Next, Louisa worked for a magazine. It was for children. She was asked to write a book about girls. Louisa knew all about the lives of girls. After all, she grew up with three sisters! So, she wrote *Little Women*. The book was set during the Civil War.

Books for children in the 1860s were often **dull**. They taught lessons about how to be good. Louisa's book was different. The March sisters got into trouble. They fought with each other. They made up. They went to parties and put on plays. They seemed real. People loved reading about them.

After the book came out, Louisa had enough money to help her family. She wrote more books about Jo March. She also wrote other stories that people loved.

Louisa bought a big house in Boston, Massachusetts, for her family. She kept writing until her death in 1888. By that time, Louisa was one of the best-loved writers in the country. Her books had sold a million copies. Today, people around the world still read Louisa's wonderful stories.

NAME: _____ DATE: _____

LOUISA MAY ALCOTT
(1832–1888)

1. Choose a good title for this story.
   a. A Well-Loved Author's Life
   b. Writing in the Nineteenth Century
   c. The Alcott Family and the March Family
   d. A Civil War Nurse

2. What does the word **dull** mean in the passage?
   a. useful
   b. boring
   c. gray
   d. simple

3. Number the following events in the order they happened.
   _____ Louisa sold a poem that she wrote.
   _____ Louisa became a nurse.
   _____ Louisa's family moved many times.
   _____ Louisa bought a house in Boston, Massachusetts.
   _____ Little Women came out and was a big success.

4. Answer the following questions.

   What job did Louisa's father have?
   _____

   When did Louisa begin to feel that she needed to earn money for her family?
   _____

   Which character in Little Women is like Louisa?
   _____

   How did Louisa earn money to help her family?
   _____
   _____

5. Why do you think Little Women was so popular?
   a. Most children's books were not fun to read at that time.
   b. The characters in Little Women seemed like real people.
   c. Louisa was a good writer.
   d. all of the above

BONUS

Write about your brother, sister, or cousin. What does this person like to do? How is he or she different from other people? What do you like about him or her? Describe a fun activity that you and the person have shared.

QUEEN LILIUOKALANI
(1838–1917)

Liliuokalani was not a queen at first. Her brother sat on the throne of Hawaii after being crowned king in 1874. Then, she was just a princess. But in 1881, the king left on a long trip and put Liliuokalani in charge of Hawaii while he was gone. The king was gone for only three weeks when disaster struck in Hawaii. A terrible **disease**, smallpox, broke out.

Liliuokalani acted quickly. She found out that some workers from China had brought the sickness to the Hawaiian Islands, so she closed the ports. Americans who shipped sugar from Hawaii were very angry. But, Liliuokalani cared only about her people and their ability to get well again.

In 1891, Liliuokalani became the queen of Hawaii. Liliuokalani was strong and independent. She was also clear about how she wanted to rule. She wanted to change the laws that Americans had forced on the islands, laws that took away her power as queen. She wanted to have that power so that she could take care of her people and give them more rights. The Americans remembered when Liliuokalani closed the ports and feared she might do that again. So, they took over. Four boatloads of soldiers marched into Honolulu, Hawaii, and arrested the queen.

President Grover Cleveland tried to stop them, but he discovered that Queen Liliuokalani planned to punish the Americans if she was released. So instead, Hawaii became a republic. In 1895, Queen Liliuokalani was jailed again and kept against her will in a room in her palace. She was held there for eight months.

Queen Liliuokalani loved music. She wrote many songs that told stories about her people and different places on the Hawaiian Islands. While she was jailed, she wrote another song, called "Aloha 'Oe." The title means "Farewell to Thee." This beautiful, sad song is about two people saying good-bye, but it is also about a queen saying good-bye to her kingdom.

Queen Liliuokalani was freed in 1896 and lived the rest of her life in Hawaii. She was the last person to rule the islands. Hawaii was made a part of the United States in 1898 and achieved statehood in 1959.

Today, Hawaiians remember Queen Liliuokalani for her strong leadership. She defended the rights of her people. And, people around the world still recognize her song "Aloha 'Oe" as one of the most familiar Hawaiian tunes.

QUEEN LILIUOKALANI
(1838–1917)

Liliuokalani was not a queen at first. Her brother became king in 1874. She was just a princess then. But in 1881, the king left on a long trip. He put Liliuokalani in charge of Hawaii while he was gone. The king was gone for only three weeks. Then, disaster struck in Hawaii. A terrible **disease**, smallpox, broke out.

Liliuokalani acted quickly. She found out that some workers from China had brought the sickness to the Hawaiian Islands. She closed the ports. Americans who shipped sugar from Hawaii were very angry. But, Liliuokalani cared only about her people. She wanted them to get well.

In 1891, Liliuokalani became the queen of Hawaii. Liliuokalani was strong. She was clear about how she wanted to rule. She wanted to change the laws that Americans had forced on the islands. These laws took away her power as a queen. She wanted to have that power back. That way, she could take care of her people. The Americans remembered when Liliuokalani closed the ports. They were afraid she might do that again. So, they took over. Four boatloads of soldiers marched into Honolulu, Hawaii. They arrested the queen.

President Grover Cleveland tried to stop them. But then, he found out that Queen Liliuokalani planned to punish the Americans if she was released. So, Hawaii became a republic. In 1895, Queen Liliuokalani was jailed again. This time, she was kept in a room in her palace. She was held there for eight months.

Queen Liliuokalani loved music. She wrote many songs. They told stories about her people. They told about different places on the islands of Hawaii. While she was jailed, she wrote another song. It is called "Aloha 'Oe." The title means "Farewell to Thee." This beautiful, sad song is about two people saying good-bye. But, it is also about a queen saying good-bye to her kingdom.

Queen Liliuokalani was freed in 1896. She lived the rest of her life in Hawaii. She was the last person to rule the islands. Hawaii was made a part of the United States in 1898. It was made a state in 1959.

Hawaiians remember Queen Liliuokalani for her strong leadership. She stood up for the rights of her people. And, people around the world still know her song "Aloha 'Oe" as one of the most familiar Hawaiian tunes.

NAME: _____ DATE: _____

QUEEN LILIUOKALANI
(1838–1917)

1. Choose a good title for this story.
   a. A Queen in Prison
   b. The History of Hawaii
   c. The Last Queen of Hawaii
   d. Americans in Hawaii

2. What does the word **disease** mean in the passage?
   a. discomfort
   b. dizziness
   c. sickness
   d. uninterested

3. Number the following events in the order they happened.
   _____ Liliuokalani wrote the song "Aloha 'Oe."
   _____ Liliuokalani became queen.
   _____ Hawaii became a republic.
   _____ Liliuokalani closed Hawaii's ports to protect the people from smallpox.
   _____ Liliuokalani's brother left her in charge of Hawaii while he was traveling.

4. Answer the following questions.
   What were Liliuokalani's songs about?
   _____
   _____

   Who ruled Hawaii before Liliuokalani?
   _____

   Where was Liliuokalani kept a prisoner?
   _____

   What laws did Liliuokalani want to change?
   _____
   _____

5. Why do you think the sugar shippers feared Liliuokalani?
   a. She did not seem like a very good queen.
   b. She closed the ports, which cost them money.
   c. They were afraid she would punish them.
   d. They wanted the people of Hawaii to be free.

BONUS

What would you need to know to rule a country? Write a paragraph telling what you think would be important to learn so that you could be a king or queen.

MARY CASSATT
(1844–1926)

Mary Cassatt told her parents that she wanted to be an artist. Her father was very upset. That was because at the time, in 1865, wealthy girls were supposed to care about art only as a hobby. They were not supposed to want jobs, not even as artists. They were never supposed to travel alone. But, Mary's parents knew that she was serious about art. And, serious artists went to France.

Paris was the center of the art world at that time. Mary studied there for five years. Then, a war broke out, and Mary had to flee Paris and go home. But, she went back as soon as she could. In Paris, Mary met many famous artists. One, named Edgar Degas, helped Mary. He told her to make paintings of mothers and children. He said that it would help people accept her work as a female artist. Mary took his **advice**.

Edgar Degas also gave Mary some colorful handmade prints from Japan. These pictures displayed many different patterns in the same scene. Mary used this idea in her own work. In one of her pictures, a woman in a dress with a pattern sits in front of a wall with patterned wallpaper and the two patterns seem to blend together.

In France, Mary became one of the most well-known artists of her time, but things were different in the United States. One time, Mary went back to visit her brother. A newspaper said that she had been "studying painting in France." This made it sound like Mary painted as a hobby. Many people felt that respectable women could not be "real" artists.

Mary knew a great deal about the painters who worked in France, and she used her knowledge to help others. She advised people in the United States about buying paintings. She also helped museums. Today, we have many great works of art in North America because Mary helped purchase them and bring them here.

Mary had to stop painting in 1914. She had trouble with her eyes and became nearly blind. Mary lived at her beloved home in the French countryside until she died in 1926. Today, her work is known around the world and her paintings sell for millions of dollars.

MARY CASSATT
(1844–1926)

Mary Cassatt wanted to be an artist. She told her parents. Her father was very upset. In 1865, girls were supposed to like art only as a hobby. They were not supposed to have jobs, even as artists. They were never supposed to travel alone. Mary's parents knew that Mary planned to do both. She wanted to learn about art. And, that meant that she wanted to go to France.

Paris was the center of the art world at that time. Mary studied there for five years. Then, a war broke out. She came home. But, she went back as soon as she could. In Paris, Mary met many well-known artists. One, named Edgar Degas, helped Mary. He told her to make paintings of mothers and children. It would help people accept her work. Mary took his **advice**.

Edgar Degas also gave Mary some handmade pictures from Japan. These pictures showed many different patterns in the same scene. Mary used this idea in her own work. In one of her pictures, a woman in a print dress sits in front of a wall with print wallpaper. The two prints blend together.

In France, Mary became one of the most well-known artists of her time. But, things were different in the United States. One time, Mary went back to visit her brother. A newspaper said that she had been "studying painting in France." This made it sound like Mary painted as a hobby. Many people still felt that women could not be "real" artists.

Mary knew a lot about the painters who worked in France. She helped people in the United States buy paintings. She also helped museums. Today, we have many great works of art in North America. Mary helped buy many of them and bring them here.

Mary had to stop painting in 1914. She had trouble with her eyes. She was nearly blind. Mary lived at her beloved home in the French countryside until she died in 1926. Today, her work is known around the world. Her paintings sell for millions of dollars.

American Women Achievers • CD-104255 • © Carson-Dellosa

NAME: _____ DATE: _____

MARY CASSATT
(1844–1926)

1. The third paragraph is mainly about:

    a. Mary's parents.
    b. Mary's work with patterns and prints.
    c. Mary's death.
    d. Mary's home in Paris.

2. What does the word **advice** mean in the passage?

    a. an article in a newspaper
    b. a tight grip
    c. a statement about a special sale
    d. an opinion about something that should be done

3. Number the following events in the order they happened.

    _____ Mary advised people and museums in the United States about buying paintings.

    _____ Mary had to leave her studies in Paris because of a war.

    _____ Mary lived her last days in her country home.

    _____ Mary told her parents that she wanted to be an artist.

    _____ Mary started to go blind.

4. Answer the following questions.

    Who was Edgar Degas?
    _____
    _____

    Why did Mary need to go to Paris?
    _____
    _____

    What help did Mary give to American museums?
    _____
    _____

    Why did Mary stop painting?
    _____
    _____

5. Why do you think Edgar Degas told Mary to paint women and children?

    a. It would make the idea of a female artist seem less strange to people.
    b. People at the time liked only paintings of women and children.
    c. Degas wanted Mary to succeed with her work.
    d. a and c

BONUS

What do you want to be when you grow up? Write about your plans.

© Carson-Dellosa • CD-104255 • American Women Achievers

JULIETTE "DAISY" GORDON LOW
(1860–1927)

The ladies at the table were astonished. A woman sat down, wearing a hat trimmed with carrots and **parsley**! The orange vegetables and green herbs drooped around her face. "Isn't my hat sad?" she asked cheerfully. "I can't afford to have it done over. I give all my money to the Girl Scouts."

The woman was Juliette Gordon Low. Everyone called her Daisy. She was from a rich and important family. She had gone to good schools and loved to travel. Daisy married a wealthy Englishman, and she went to live with him in England but would come back to the United States to visit her family.

Daisy had lost almost all of her hearing by 1886. She never let that slow her down. She helped her mother start a hospital, she toured India, and she went to live in Paris, France, for a time after her husband died. But, Daisy longed to do something special with her life.

In 1911, she met Sir Robert Baden-Powell, the man who started the Boy Scouts and the Girl Guides in England. Daisy was interested to learn about his groups and the values they taught. Then, Daisy traveled home and called one of her cousins. She said that she had something for all of the girls in America and she was going to start it that very night! On March 12, 1912, Daisy founded the first Girl Scout troop in the United States with 18 girls as members.

After that, Daisy worked night and day for the Girl Scouts. She held meetings, raised money, and used all sorts of stunts to get people to help with her group. One time, she stood on her head at a meeting. Why? She wanted to show off the new shoes for the Girl Scouts uniform!

Daisy even made her hearing problem useful. When someone said that she did not have any money to give to the Girl Scouts, Daisy would pretend she could not hear her.

Girls in the United States did not have a lot of choices at that time. They often did not have much education, and most girls got married and took care of families. Daisy wanted girls to have more opportunities. The Girl Scouts helped girls learn about the arts and sciences and encouraged girls to spend healthy time outdoors. Unlike many groups of the time, the Scouts accepted girls who had special challenges, like Daisy's hearing problem. It gave all girls the chance to learn and grow.

Today, there are 3.7 million Girl Scouts who can thank Juliette Gordon Low for founding their organization. Daisy would be amazed and proud to see what her hard work has accomplished.

JULIETTE "DAISY" GORDON LOW
(1860–1927)

The ladies at the table were astonished. A woman sat down. She was wearing a hat trimmed with carrots and **parsley**! The orange vegetables and green herbs drooped around her face. "Isn't my hat sad?" she asked cheerfully. "I can't afford to have it done over. I give all my money to the Girl Scouts."

The woman was Juliette Gordon Low. Everyone called her Daisy. She was from a rich family. She had gone to good schools. She loved to travel. Daisy married a wealthy Englishman. She lived in England but would come back to the United States to see her family.

Daisy had lost almost all of her hearing by 1886. She never let that slow her down. She helped her mother start a hospital. She went to India. She lived in Paris, France, after her husband died. But, Daisy longed to do something special with her life.

In 1911, she met the man who started the Boy Scouts and the Girl Guides in England. His name was Sir Robert Baden-Powell. Daisy wanted to learn about his groups. Daisy went home. She called her cousin. She told her that she had something for all of the girls in America and she was going to start it that night! On March 12, 1912, Daisy started the first Girl Scout troop in the United States with 18 girls.

After that, Daisy worked night and day for the Girl Scouts. She held meetings. She raised money. She did all sorts of things to get people to help with her group. One time, she stood on her head at a meeting. Why? She wanted to show off the new shoes for the Girl Scouts uniform!

Daisy even made her hearing problem useful. When someone said that she did not have any money to give to the Girl Scouts, Daisy would pretend she could not hear her.

Girls in the United States did not have a lot of choices at that time. They often did not have much schooling. Most girls got married and took care of families. Daisy wanted girls to have more choices. The Girl Scouts helped girls learn about the arts and sciences. It helped girls spend healthy time outdoors. And, the Scouts accepted girls with special challenges, like Daisy's hearing problem. It gave all girls the chance to learn and grow.

Today, there are 3.7 million Girl Scouts. Daisy would be amazed and proud to see what her hard work has done.

NAME: _____ DATE: _____

JULIETTE "DAISY" GORDON LOW
(1860–1927)

1. The fourth paragraph is mainly about:

    a. how Daisy lost her hearing.

    b. Daisy's childhood.

    c. how Daisy started the Girl Scouts.

    d. Daisy's marriage.

2. What does the word **parsley** mean in the passage?

    a. a leafy green herb

    b. a type of hat

    c. a fruit

    d. a type of tree

3. Number the following events in the order they happened.

    _____ Daisy started the first Girl Scout troop.

    _____ Daisy lost most of her hearing.

    _____ Daisy learned about the Boy Scouts and the Girl Guides.

    _____ Daisy's husband died.

    _____ Daisy was born into a rich family.

4. Answer the following questions.

    What physical problem did Daisy have?

    _____

    _____

    Who was Sir Robert Baden-Powell?

    _____

    _____

    Where did Daisy live after her wedding?

    _____

    How many Girl Scouts were there in the first troop?

    _____

5. Why does the author say that it was important for Daisy to start the Girl Scouts?

    a. It taught girls how to be good housewives.

    b. It taught girls that they had many choices of things to do with their lives.

    c. It accepted girls who had special challenges, like hearing problems.

    d. b and c

BONUS

Pretend that you want to start a group to help people. Write a plan showing what steps you will take. Whom will your group help? What will your group be called?

MARY McLEOD BETHUNE
(1875–1955)

Mary McLeod Bethune grew up in a poor family. She had 16 brothers and sisters who all lived together in a tiny log cabin. They worked together, picking cotton. While she worked, Mary watched white children walk to school each day, and she longed to go with them.

Mary's mother and father had been slaves, and Mary's mother still worked for her former owners. One day, she took Mary with her. At the house, Mary picked up a book and one of the little girls from the family took it away from her. "You can't read that," she told Mary and gave her a picture book instead. But from that moment, Mary was **determined** that she would learn how to read.

Not long after that, Mary got her chance. A church opened a small mission school five miles from Mary's house. Mary learned everything that she could. Then, she came home and taught what she had learned to her family and friends. It was thrilling for her family to sit and listen to Mary read to them, because nobody else in her family had ever been given the chance to learn.

When Mary was 16 years old, she finished school. She went back to work in the cotton fields. But then, another big chance came to her. The teachers at her school had sent her name to a school in North Carolina, and Mary was offered a free place at the school. Mary loved being at school again. She decided that she was going to open a school of her own so that she could give other black girls the same chance that she had been given.

Mary went to Florida in 1899, arriving there with only a dollar and a half! But, she forged ahead. She started her school in one room with five students. Mary made the benches and stools for the students herself. But by 1923, the school had become a college. It merged with a boy's school, becoming Bethune-Cookman College, and is still open today.

Mary became an important voice for African Americans. She fought for equal rights. She helped the Red Cross increase the number of black volunteers. She became an advisor to several presidents. She also started the National Council of Negro Women, a group that acted as a guide on important issues for black people.

Mary greatly admired her mother and once said that no matter what happened, her mother thought that everything would work out for the best. Mary used that same feeling as a compass to find her way through life. And, her life changed the lives of thousands of others as she worked to make the world better for African Americans.

MARY McLEOD BETHUNE
(1875–1955)

Mary McLeod Bethune grew up in a poor family. She had 16 brothers and sisters. They all lived together in a tiny log cabin. They worked together, picking cotton. While she worked, Mary watched white children walk to school each day. She longed to go with them.

Mary's mother and father had been slaves. Mary's mother still worked for her former owners. One day, she took Mary with her. Mary picked up a book. One of the little girls in the house took it away from her. "You can't read that," she told Mary. She gave her a picture book instead. But from that moment, Mary was **determined** that she would learn how to read.

Not long after that, Mary got her chance. A small school opened five miles from Mary's house. Mary learned everything that she could. Then, she came home and taught what she had learned to her family and friends. It was thrilling for her family to sit and listen to Mary read to them. Nobody else in her family had ever gone to school.

When Mary was 16 years old, she finished school. She went back to work in the cotton fields. But then, another big chance came to her. The teachers at her school sent her name to a school in North Carolina. Mary went for free. Mary loved being at school again. She wanted to open a school of her own. She wanted to give other black girls the same chance that she had been given.

Mary moved to Florida. When she got there in 1899, she had only a dollar and a half! But, she kept going. Her school was one room. She had five students. Mary made the benches and stools for the students herself. But by 1923, the school had become a college. It merged with a boy's school. It became Bethune-Cookman College. This school is still open today.

Mary became an important voice for African Americans. She fought for equal rights. She helped the Red Cross find more black people to join and help. She gave advice to several presidents. She started the National Council of Negro Women. This group acted as a guide on important issues for black people.

Mary admired her mother. She once said that no matter what happened, her mother felt that everything would work out for the best. Mary used that same feeling to find her way through life. And, her life changed the lives of thousands of others as she worked to make the world better for African Americans.

American Women Achievers • CD-104255 • © Carson-Dellosa

NAME: _____   DATE: _____

MARY McLEOD BETHUNE
(1875–1955)

1. Choose a good title for this story.

   a. Determined to Learn, Determined to Teach

   b. Former Slaves Go to School

   c. One Great Chance

   d. Learning to Read

2. What does the word **determined** mean in the passage?

   a. judged

   b. kept something from happening

   c. dug up the truth

   d. was sure about doing something

3. Number the following events in the order they happened.

   _____ Mary got a free place at a school in North Carolina.

   _____ Mary went to a small school near her home.

   _____ Mary started the National Council of Negro Women.

   _____ Mary started teaching in her own school.

   _____ Mary went to work with her mother.

4. Answer the following questions.

   What school did Mary McLeod Bethune start?

   _____

   How many students did she have in her first class as a teacher?

   _____

   How many brothers and sisters did Mary have?

   _____

   What happened that made Mary certain that she had to learn how to read?

   _____

   _____

5. Why did Mary feel that it was so important for her to open a school?

   a. She wanted to do more teaching after teaching people in her family.

   b. She needed a job and thought that teaching would be a good job.

   c. She wanted to give other African American girls the same chance that she had.

   d. none of the above

BONUS

Draw a picture of a classroom where you would like to learn. Then, write about what you would need to make or buy to improve your real classroom.

© Carson-Dellosa • CD-104255 • American Women Achievers

HELEN KELLER
(1880–1968)

When baby Helen got sick, the doctor did not think that she would live. The Keller family was worried and scared. Helen did get better, but something was wrong. She no longer responded to voices or lights. Helen Keller, not yet two years old, was both blind and deaf.

The next few years were terrible for the Keller family. Helen acted like a wild animal. Nobody could talk to her or help her. She screamed, broke dishes, and turned over chairs. She was thought to be unteachable, but Helen's parents wanted to help her. They met with Alexander Graham Bell, who was interested in working with deaf children. He helped the Kellers find a teacher for Helen, a woman named Anne Sullivan.

Anne came to live with the Keller family in 1886. She tried to teach Helen how to fingerspell words. She would give Helen a doll or a cookie, then spell the word in the girl's hand. Helen was good at repeating the finger movements, but she did not know what they meant. It was not until a day in April 1887 that Anne broke through to Helen's world with a single word: *water*.

Anne pumped water into Helen's hand and spelled the word *water* at the same time. This might have been a word that Helen had known as a baby or it might have been Anne's tireless work that caused the breakthrough. Nobody knows for sure. But suddenly, Helen understood that the finger movements were words, and the words were telling her about the world. By the end of that day, Helen had learned 30 new words!

Helen kept learning fast. Anne was able to teach Helen how to read braille and how to write. She was not only teachable, but she was also very intelligent. By 1900, Helen was able to go to college.

In 1903, Helen wrote her first book, which told the story of her early life. Helen was able to buy a house with the money that she made from this book, and she went on to write 10 more books. With her books and speeches, Helen also raised money to help people who were struggling because they could not see or hear.

Anne Sullivan stayed with Helen for the rest of her life. The two women toured the world, visiting 39 different countries. Helen gave talks that Anne translated. Helen's work gave hope to people around the world. She and Anne Sullivan created a way to teach the blind and deaf that is still used today. When Helen came out of her dark world, she became a **beacon** for others, to show them the way.

HELEN KELLER
(1880–1968)

When baby Helen got sick, the doctor did not think that she would live. The Keller family was worried and scared. Helen did get better, but something was wrong. She no longer heard voices or saw lights. Helen Keller, not yet two years old, was both blind and deaf.

The next few years were terrible for the Keller family. Helen was like a wild animal. Nobody could talk to her or help her. She screamed, broke dishes, and turned over chairs. She was thought to be unteachable. But, Helen's parents wanted to help her. They met with Alexander Graham Bell. He was interested in working with deaf children. He helped the Kellers find a teacher for Helen. The teacher's name was Anne Sullivan.

Anne came to live with the Keller family in 1886. She tried to teach Helen how to fingerspell words. She would give Helen a doll or a cookie. Then, she would spell the word in the girl's hand. Helen was good at repeating the finger movements. But, she did not know what they meant. It was not until a day in April 1887 that Anne broke through to Helen's world with a single word: *water*.

Anne pumped water into Helen's hand and spelled the word *water*. This might have been a word that Helen knew as a baby. Or, it might have been Anne's tireless work that caused the breakthrough. Nobody knows for sure. But suddenly, Helen knew that the finger movements were words. The words were telling her about the world. By the end of that day, Helen had learned 30 new words!

Helen kept learning fast. Anne was able to teach Helen how to read braille. She learned to write. She was not only teachable, but she was also very smart. By 1900, Helen was able to go to college.

In 1903, Helen wrote her first book. It told the story of her early life. Helen was able to buy a house with the money that she made from this book. She went on to write 10 more books. With her books and speeches, Helen raised money to help people who could not see or hear.

Anne Sullivan stayed with Helen for the rest of her life. The two women toured the world. They visited 39 different countries. Helen gave talks. Anne translated. Helen's work gave hope to people around the world. She and Anne Sullivan created a way to teach the blind and deaf that is still used today. When Helen came out of her dark world, she became a **beacon** for others, to show them the way.

NAME: _____ DATE: _____

HELEN KELLER
(1880–1968)

1. Choose a good title for this story.

   a. Anne Sullivan, Teacher

   b. A Childhood Illness

   c. Helen Keller, Author

   d. The Struggle Back to the Light

2. What does the word **beacon** mean in the passage?

   a. a bird's bill

   b. an inspiring light

   c. a type of flashlight

   d. a type of glass container

3. Number the following events in the order they happened.

   _____ Helen became blind and deaf.

   _____ Anne Sullivan went to live with the Keller family.

   _____ Helen learned to read braille.

   _____ Helen traveled with Anne around the world.

   _____ Helen Keller wrote her first book.

4. Answer the following questions.

   What happened to Helen Keller as a baby?
   _____
   _____

   Who was Anne Sullivan?
   _____
   _____

   Where did Helen go in 1900?
   _____

   How did Anne Sullivan teach words to Helen Keller?
   _____
   _____

5. Helen Keller said that the most important day of her life was the day that Anne Sullivan came to live with her family. Why do you think she felt that way?

   a. Anne was sent by Alexander Graham Bell, who was a very important man.

   b. Without Anne, Helen may have never learned how to talk, write, or learn.

   c. Anne became one of Helen's best friends.

   d. Helen's parents did not care what happened to her, but Anne did.

BONUS

Imagine a person who suddenly could not see or hear. What would that person miss the most? What everyday things would become hard to do? Write a paragraph about it.

---

46   American Women Achievers • CD-104255 • © Carson-Dellosa

JEANNETTE RANKIN
(1880–1973)

The "Tin Lizzie," a battered Model T Ford, came slowly down the muddy road. The rancher's children had never seen an automobile before and ran to it. A woman was driving! She got out of the car. "Are your parents at home?" she asked. "My name is Jeannette Rankin."

Running for Congress in Montana was not an easy task. It was a huge state with few good roads. But, Jeannette knew that she had to talk to people face-to-face in order to get their votes. She had to explain to them why a woman should be elected to Congress for the first time in history.

Jeannette knew Montana well, because she was born on a small ranch near the Montana town of Grant. Her mother worked as a teacher. Jeannette went to college, then was employed for a time as a social worker. But later, she started working for women's right to vote and knew that she had found what she wanted to do with her life—work for the good of others through politics.

Jeannette was elected to the House of Representatives in 1916. She wanted to convince Congress to give the vote to all women, she wanted to keep child laborers out of factories, and she wanted to keep the United States out of the coming war.

Jeannette had served for only four days when the vote for war came to the floor of Congress. Should the United States enter World War I? Jeannette voted no. So did 55 of the male members of Congress, but the press focused on Jeannette's vote. People were angry and said that her choice proved that women were too weak to serve in the government. Jeannette ran for the Senate in 1918 but did not win.

That did not stop her. She spent the next 20 years working for peace. She lived part of that time in Georgia and part of that time in Montana, but she spent most of her time in Washington, D.C. She gave many speeches, founded the Georgia Peace Society, and became more and more certain that peace was the best avenue for all countries.

In the 1930s, war started to loom again. In 1939, Jeannette went home to Montana, ran for Congress, and won in 1940. In 1941, Pearl Harbor was bombed. Congress had to vote on whether to enter World War II.

Many people thought that the United States had no choice because the country had been attacked, but Jeannette would not back down. She was the only member of Congress to vote against entering World War II. She said, "As a woman, I can't go to war, and I **refuse** to send anyone else." After her term was over, she did not run for office again.

Jeannette spent the rest of her life working for world peace. When she was almost 90 years old, she led a protest against the Vietnam War. All of her life, she knew in her heart that peace was the best way.

JEANNETTE RANKIN
(1880–1973)

The "Tin Lizzie," a Model T Ford, came slowly down the muddy road. The rancher's children had never seen a car before. They ran to it. A woman was driving! She got out of the car. "Are your parents at home?" she asked. "My name is Jeannette Rankin."

Running for Congress in Montana was not easy. It is a huge state. There were few good roads. But, Jeannette knew that she had to talk to people face-to-face. She had to explain to them why a woman should be sent to Congress for the first time in history.

Jeannette knew Montana well. She was born on a small ranch near the Montana town of Grant. Her mother worked as a teacher. Jeannette went to college. She worked for a time as a social worker. But then, she started working for women's right to vote. She knew that she had found what she wanted to do with her life—work for the good of others through politics.

Jeannette was elected to the House of Representatives in 1916. She wanted Congress to give the vote to all women in the country. She wanted to keep child workers out of factories. And, she wanted to keep the United States out of the coming war.

Jeannette had been in Congress for only four days when the vote for war came. Should the United States fight in World War I? Jeannette voted no. So did 55 of the male members of Congress. But, the press wrote mostly about Jeannette's vote. People were angry. They said that her choice proved that women were too weak to serve in the government. Jeannette ran for the Senate in 1918. She did not win.

That did not stop her. She spent the next 20 years working for peace. She lived part of that time in Georgia. She lived part of that time in Montana. But, she spent most of her time in Washington, D.C. She gave many speeches. She founded the Georgia Peace Society. She became more and more sure that peace was the best choice for all countries.

In the 1930s, war started to loom again. Jeannette went home to Montana. She ran for Congress in 1940 and won. In 1941, Pearl Harbor was bombed. Congress had to vote on whether to enter World War II.

Many people thought that the United States had no choice. The country had been attacked. But, Jeannette would not back down. She was the only member of Congress to vote against going to war. She said, "As a woman, I can't go to war, and I **refuse** to send anyone else." After her term was over, she did not run again.

Jeannette spent the rest of her life working for world peace. When she was almost 90 years old, she led a protest against the Vietnam War. All of her life, she knew in her heart that peace was the best way.

NAME: _____ DATE: _____

JEANNETTE RANKIN
(1880–1973)

1. This story tells about:

   a. a woman who was a schoolteacher.

   b. a woman who wanted to live a quiet life.

   c. the first woman to be a social worker.

   d. the first woman to serve in Congress.

2. What does the word **refuse** mean in the passage?

   a. garbage

   b. to be unwilling

   c. to be eager

   d. a string that sets off an explosion

3. Number the following events in the order they happened.

   _____ Jeannette was born on a ranch near the town of Grant, Montana.

   _____ Jeannette led a protest against the Vietnam War.

   _____ Jeannette voted against going to war in 1941.

   _____ Jeannette worked as a social worker.

   _____ Jeannette ran for Congress in 1916.

4. Answer the following questions.

   What is a "Tin Lizzie"?

   _____

   _____

   In what state was Jeannette Rankin born?

   _____

   What cause did Jeannette work for her whole life?

   _____

   Why did Jeannette vote against entering World War II?

   _____

   _____

5. Why do you think the press wrote about Jeannette's vote against World War I?

   a. She was the first woman in Congress, and her vote was big news.

   b. Some people thought that women were not strong enough to vote for war.

   c. Everyone approved of Jeannette's vote.

   d. a and b

BONUS

Pretend that you are Jeannette Rankin. Write a short speech explaining something about which you feel strongly.

© Carson-Dellosa • CD-104255 • American Women Achievers

ELEANOR ROOSEVELT
(1884–1962)

Eleanor Roosevelt was the First Lady of the United States for four presidential terms. She came to the White House as the wife of President Franklin D. Roosevelt. But, she was much more than the president's wife. She made the **role** of First Lady into something new. She became an important part of American politics, instead of just being the president's wife and hostess.

Eleanor was the niece of President Theodore Roosevelt. Even though she came from a famous family, she was shy as a young girl. Then, she was sent to school in England. She learned that she was a leader. Other girls looked up to her as a good writer, a good athlete, and a good friend.

In 1905, Eleanor married Franklin, a charming and good-looking young man. He went into politics, but in 1921, something terrible happened. Franklin became sick with polio, a crippling disease. Eleanor and Franklin had five children. She had to take care of them, as well as Franklin. Franklin got better, but he never fully recovered. He spent most of his time after that in a wheelchair.

Eleanor became his "eyes and ears." She traveled and gave speeches, helping Franklin find out what he needed to know for his work. They became a team, working together both before and after Franklin became president.

After Franklin was elected president in 1932, Eleanor and Franklin moved into the White House. Eleanor worked very hard as First Lady, focusing on civil rights. She also worked for laws to help American workers and improve life for the poor.

Eleanor was a strong voice for women's rights. When she was First Lady, she let only female reporters interview her, knowing that newspapers would have to hire women if they wanted the full story from the White House. And, they did.

Because Franklin could not travel, Eleanor made trips on his behalf. She went down into coal mines and to the tops of skyscrapers. She visited cities and towns across the country and even traveled fearlessly to war zones to speak to soldiers during World War II.

Franklin died in 1945, but Eleanor continued working for the American people. She was given a place as spokesperson at the United Nations. She helped write a declaration for human rights and spoke in many countries about that cause. She also wrote for newspapers across the country. She supported many different causes until her death in 1962. Her life and her care for people changed the lives of many Americans, making her one of the most loved First Ladies of all time.

ELEANOR ROOSEVELT
(1884–1962)

Eleanor Roosevelt was the First Lady of the United States for four presidential terms. She was the wife of President Franklin D. Roosevelt. But, she was much more than that. She made the **role** of First Lady into something new. She became an important part of American politics, instead of just being the president's wife and hostess.

Eleanor was the niece of President Theodore Roosevelt. She was shy as a young girl. Then, she was sent to school in England. She learned that she was a leader. Other girls looked up to her. She was a good writer, a good athlete, and a good friend.

In 1905, Eleanor married Franklin. He was charming and good-looking. He went into politics. But in 1921, something terrible happened. Franklin got polio. This was a crippling disease. Eleanor and Franklin had five children. She had to take care of them and Franklin at the same time. Franklin got better. But, he spent most of his time in a wheelchair.

Eleanor became his "eyes and ears." She traveled and gave speeches. She helped Franklin find out what he needed to know for his work. They became a team. They worked together both before and after Franklin became president.

In 1932, Franklin was elected president. Eleanor and Franklin moved into the White House. Eleanor worked very hard as First Lady. She worked for civil rights. She worked for laws to help American workers. She helped improve life for the poor.

Eleanor also worked for women's rights. When she was First Lady, she let only female reporters speak with her. She knew that newspapers would have to hire women if they wanted the full story from the White House. And, they did.

Because Franklin could not travel, Eleanor made trips for him. She went down into coal mines. She went to the tops of skyscrapers. She visited cities and towns across the country. She even went to war zones to speak to soldiers during World War II.

Franklin died in 1945. But, Eleanor kept working for the American people. She worked as a part of the United Nations. She helped write a declaration for human rights. She spoke in many countries. She wrote for newspapers across the country. She worked for many different causes until her death in 1962. Her life and her care for people changed the lives of many Americans. Eleanor is one of the most loved First Ladies of all time.

NAME: _____ DATE: _____

ELEANOR ROOSEVELT
(1884–1962)

1. The second paragraph is mainly about:

    a. Eleanor's time in school and how it changed her.

    b. Eleanor's marriage.

    c. Eleanor's work during World War II.

    d. Eleanor's parents.

2. What does the word **role** mean in the passage?

    a. a round piece of bread

    b. to move down a slant by rolling

    c. a part to play

    d. boiling hot

3. Number the following events in the order they happened.

    _____ Eleanor cared for Franklin when he got polio.

    _____ Eleanor worked for human rights at the United Nations.

    _____ Eleanor married Franklin.

    _____ Eleanor visited soldiers during World War II.

    _____ Eleanor and Franklin moved into the White House.

4. Answer the following questions.

    How did Eleanor's school days in England change her?

    _____
    _____

    How did Eleanor help Franklin while he was president?

    _____
    _____

    Who was Eleanor's uncle?

    _____

    What was different about the way that Eleanor worked as First Lady?

    _____
    _____

5. What was one way that Eleanor helped women?

    a. She would not hire men to work in her home.

    b. She would not let male reporters interview her.

    c. She did not let men have jobs at the United Nations.

    d. She wrote novels about women.

BONUS

What do you think was the most important cause that Eleanor supported? Write a paragraph about it. Be sure to tell why you think it was important.

MARY PICKFORD
(1892–1979)

Little Gladys Smith was six years old when her father died. Her mother did not have any money to support her family. So, she rented rooms in her house to boarders. She took in sewing. And, she let Gladys act. The child's first part was in a Toronto, Canada, stage play called *The Silver King*. Gladys was only seven years old, but she was a big hit.

The little girl dreamed of acting in New York City, New York. She went there when she was 15 and got a part in a play on Broadway. She changed her name to Mary Pickford.

Mary was very savvy about acting. She saw that people were starting to make movies and knew that it would be a good way to make money. She went to see a director named D. W. Griffith, who told Mary that he would pay her $5 a day. Mary told him that she was already an actress on the stage, so she would require $10 a day. He agreed.

Soon, Mary was making dozens of short movies. Directors started making longer, or "feature length," films. By 1916, Mary had made 21 of these new, longer movies. People loved her on the screen. At this time, many families in North America made about $1,500 a year, but Mary made 100 times that much money!

In 1917, Mary tried something new. She made two movies in which she played children. The other actors in the movies were chosen because they were very tall, or they stood on boxes. The furniture was oversized, so Mary looked very small. People loved these movies. Later, though, Mary wished that she had not made them. Now, people wanted to see Mary play only the part of a young girl.

Mary was smart about investing money. In 1919, she was ready to make another big move, using her money to **found** a movie company with three other people. The company was called United Artists.

In 1927, she helped start the Academy of Motion Picture Arts and Sciences. This group gives out the most important awards in the movie industry: the Oscars®.

Mary wanted to keep acting, but when she was 40 years old, she could no longer play the children and teenagers that people wanted to see. She tried to play adult parts, but they were not well received. So, she stopped acting in 1933.

Mary played a vital role in one of the biggest new businesses in the world: the making of movies. Today, people still enjoy her acting and the film academy that she helped create.

MARY PICKFORD
(1892–1979)

Little Gladys Smith was six years old when her father died. Her mother did not have any money. She rented out rooms in her house. She sewed. And, she let Gladys act. The child's first part was in a stage play in Toronto, Canada. It was called *The Silver King*. Gladys was only seven years old. She was a big hit.

The little girl wanted to act in New York City, New York. She went there when she was 15. She got a part in a play on Broadway. She changed her name to Mary Pickford.

Mary was very smart about acting. She saw that people were starting to make movies. She knew that it would be a good way to make money. She went to see a director named D. W. Griffith. He told Mary that he would pay her $5 a day. Mary told him that she was already an actress on the stage. She wanted to get paid $10 a day. He agreed.

Soon, Mary was making dozens of short movies. Then, directors started making longer films. They were called "feature length" movies. By 1916, Mary had made 21 of these new, longer films. People loved her on the screen. At this time, many families in North America made about $1,500 a year. Mary made 100 times that much money!

In 1917, Mary tried something new. She made two movies in which she played children. The other actors in the movies were very tall or stood on boxes. The furniture was built big so that Mary looked very small. People loved these movies. Later, though, Mary wished that she had not made them. Now, people wanted to see Mary play only the part of a young girl.

Mary was smart with money. In 1919, she was ready to make another big move. She used her money to **found** a movie company with three other people. The company was called United Artists.

In 1927, she helped start the Academy of Motion Picture Arts and Sciences. This group gives out the most important awards in the movies: the Oscars®.

Mary wanted to keep acting. But when she was 40 years old, she could not play the children and teenagers that people wanted to see. She tried to play grown-up parts, but it did not work. So, she stopped acting in 1933.

Mary played a part in one of the biggest new businesses in the world: the making of movies. Today, people still enjoy her acting and the film academy that she helped create.

NAME: _____ DATE: _____

MARY PICKFORD
(1892–1979)

1. Choose a good title for this story.

   a. The Child Actor

   b. A Creative Career in the Movies

   c. The Start of United Artists

   d. Mary Pickford's Dream of Broadway

2. What does the word **found** mean in the passage?

   a. started or created

   b. discovered

   c. uncovered

   d. stalled

3. Number the following events in the order they happened.

   _____ Mary decided to stop acting.

   _____ Mary started a movie company with three other people.

   _____ Mary helped start the group that gives out the Oscars®.

   _____ Mary got her first job making movies.

   _____ Mary made her first two movies in which she played children.

4. Answer the following questions.

   What did Mary Pickford's parents name her?
   _____

   What was Mary Pickford's first acting job?
   _____
   _____

   Who was D. W. Griffith?
   _____
   _____

   What was the name of Mary's movie company?
   _____

5. Why did Mary later wish that she had not made her "child" movies?

   a. She could not play young children and teenagers forever.

   b. It limited the kinds of parts she could play in movies.

   c. It forced her to stop acting earlier than she wanted to.

   d. all of the above

BONUS

What is the best movie you have ever seen? Write a paragraph about it.

AMELIA EARHART
(1897–1937)

It was not surprising that Amelia Earhart wanted to fly an airplane. As a little girl, she was fearless about everything, sledding down the steepest hills and climbing the highest trees. But in the early days of airplanes, few women flew planes. Amelia did not let that stop her. She knew, after her first flight in 1920, that she wanted to be a pilot.

Amelia began flying lessons in 1921. After saving her money for six months, she bought her first plane. It was yellow, and Amelia named it *Canary*. She kept working to earn money and practiced flying at air meets. In 1922, she set a record for the highest altitude in a flight by a woman.

Then in 1928, Amelia got a phone call from a man named Hilton H. Railey. He asked her if she could cross the Atlantic Ocean in a plane. Amelia said that she could. Charles Lindbergh was the first man to fly across the Atlantic, and Amelia became the first woman to do so. After her flight, people called her "Lady Lindy." In 1932, Amelia flew across the Atlantic again. This time, she flew solo. In 1935, she was the first person to fly alone from Hawaii to California. She kept setting records, but in 1937, she made the biggest news of all. Amelia announced that she was going to fly around the world.

Amelia chose her navigator, a man named Fred Noonan. They took off on their flight on June 1, 1937, departing from Florida. Her friends never dreamed it would be the last time that they ever saw Amelia.

By July 2, Amelia and Fred were flying over the Pacific Ocean. They planned to land on a tiny island. It was supposed to be a sunny, clear day, but it was not. A ship picked up a radio transmission from Amelia. She reported that she was getting low on gas. She and Fred could not see the island or the ship. That was the last information ever heard from Amelia Earhart.

President Roosevelt called for a widespread search for Amelia's plane. Millions of dollars were spent trying to find the lost pilot and navigator. The search lasted two weeks, but there was no trace of Amelia, Fred, or their plane. They **vanished**.

We may never find the truth about the death of this brave female pilot. But, Amelia proved that women could play a part in opening up a brand-new field like aviation. Amelia showed that women could have the same jobs as men and succeed.

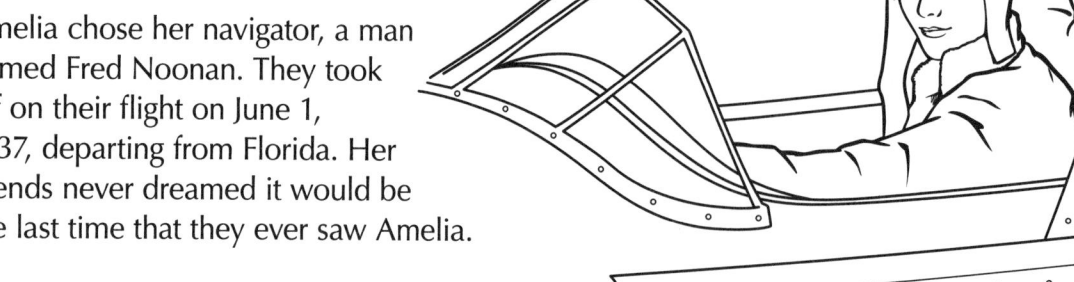

AMELIA EARHART
(1897–1937)

It was not surprising that Amelia Earhart wanted to fly an airplane. As a little girl, she was fearless about everything. She sledded down the steepest hills. She climbed the highest trees. But, few women flew planes. Amelia did not let that stop her. After her first flight in 1920, she knew that she wanted to be a pilot.

Amelia started flying lessons in 1921. She saved her money for six months. Then, she bought her first plane. It was yellow. Amelia named it *Canary*. She kept working but flew at air meets. In 1922, she set a record for the highest flight by a woman.

Then in 1928, she got a phone call from a man named Hilton H. Railey. He asked her if she could cross the Atlantic Ocean in a plane. Amelia said that she could. Charles Lindbergh was the first man to fly across the sea in a plane. Amelia became the first woman to do so. After her flight, people called her "Lady Lindy." In 1932, Amelia flew across the Atlantic again. This time, she flew alone. In 1935, she was the first person to fly alone from Hawaii to California. She kept setting records. But in 1937, she made the biggest news of all. Amelia was going to fly around the world.

Amelia picked her navigator. He was a man named Fred Noonan. Amelia and Fred took off on their flight on June 1, 1937. They left from Florida. Her friends never dreamed it would be the last time that they ever saw Amelia.

By July 2, Amelia and Fred were flying over the Pacific Ocean. They planned to land on a tiny island. It was supposed to be a sunny day. It was not. A ship picked up a radio call from Amelia. She said that she was getting low on gas. She and Fred could not see the island or the ship. No one ever heard from Amelia again.

President Roosevelt called for a search for Amelia's plane. Millions of dollars were spent trying to find the lost pilot and navigator. The search lasted two weeks. But, there was no trace of Amelia, Fred, or their plane. They **vanished**.

We may never find the truth about the death of this brave female pilot. But, Amelia proved that women could help open up a brand-new field like flight. Amelia showed that women could have the same jobs as men and do well.

NAME: _____ DATE: _____

AMELIA EARHART
(1897–1937)

1. The third paragraph is mostly about:

    a. Amelia's flight around the world.

    b. different records that Amelia set.

    c. how Amelia learned to fly.

    d. why Amelia's life was important.

2. What does the word **vanished** mean in the passage?

    a. appeared

    b. defeated

    c. derailed

    d. disappeared

3. Number the following events in the order they happened.

    _____ A search was made to try to find Amelia.

    _____ Amelia rode in a plane for the first time.

    _____ Amelia flew from Hawaii to California.

    _____ Amelia bought a plane.

    _____ Amelia crossed the Atlantic Ocean on her own.

4. Answer the following questions.

    What was *Canary*?
    _____

    Who was Fred Noonan?
    _____
    _____

    When did Amelia Earhart go on her first flight?
    _____

    What was Amelia doing on July 2, 1937?
    _____
    _____

5. Why do you think people called Amelia "Lady Lindy"?

    a. She was Charles Lindbergh's cousin.

    b. She was a pilot, like Charles Lindbergh, but she was a woman.

    c. She flew the same kind of plane that Charles Lindbergh did.

    d. She knew a dance called "the Lindy."

BONUS

If you flew around the world, what places would you want to see? Where would you like to stop and visit? Write a story about it.

MARGARET BOURKE-WHITE
(1904–1971)

When Margaret Bourke-White was little, she pretended to take pictures with a cigar box "camera." Her father had a real camera and loved to take photos. Margaret helped her father **develop** film in the family's bathtub and turn it into pictures. It seemed clear what she would do as an adult.

In 1921, Margaret went to college, but she did not think about photography as a career. She took pictures for the yearbook. She studied other subjects, but nothing except photography interested her. So, she opened her own studio. She took pictures of houses and gardens during the day, but she went to steel mills, factories, and plants at night. She loved to take pictures of people at work. One of her best-known early pictures was of a dam being built in Montana.

The Soviet Union was trying to improve its factories and industry. The country would not allow people from many other countries to enter. But after showing the Soviets her work, Margaret was allowed to come and take photographs. She wrote articles about her travels in the Soviet Union. She took pictures of the machines and the people.

Next, Margaret came home and took pictures of people in the United States. The Great Depression in the 1930s left thousands of people without homes and food. Margaret traveled with a writer named Erskine Caldwell. They took pictures of poor people in the South.

Margaret was given a job at a new magazine called *Life*, which featured a new kind of article called a photo essay. A photo essay is a story told through photographs. It was perfect for Margaret. She traveled around the United States and Europe, taking photos and writing. During World War II, Margaret went back to the Soviet Union. She and Erskine were the only American reporters there when the German army attacked.

Margaret became the first female war reporter. She took important photos of battles in Italy and Africa. She flew on raids and took pictures from the planes. She was with General Patton's army when it freed prisoners from a concentration camp at the end of the war.

After the war, Margaret kept traveling. She went to Africa. She went to India. She always helped important causes with her photos. Her pictures help us see history as if we were there. Her work is a lasting gift to people all around the world.

MARGARET BOURKE-WHITE
(1904–1971)

As a little girl, Margaret Bourke-White pretended to take pictures. She had a "camera" made from a cigar box. Her father had a real camera. She helped her father **develop** film in their bathtub. They turned the film into pictures. It seemed clear what Margaret would do when she grew up.

But, she did not think of photos as a way to make a living at first. Margaret Bourke-White went to college in 1921. She took pictures for the yearbook. She tried to study other things, but nothing interested her. So, she opened a studio. She took pictures of houses and gardens during the day. During the night, she went to factories and took pictures. She loved taking pictures of people working. She loved factories, mills, and plants. One of her most famous pictures is of a dam being built in Montana.

She wanted to go to another country to take pictures. The Soviet Union was trying to make its factories and industry better. Most people were not allowed to go into the country. But, Margaret showed the Soviets her pictures of working people. They let her enter the country. She took pictures and wrote about her travels there.

Margaret came home to the United States. In the 1930s, many people lost their jobs. Poor people were barely able to live. Margaret went to the South to take photos. She worked with a writer named Erskine Caldwell.

Margaret was given a new job. It was with a magazine called *Life*. The magazine had a lot of pictures. It printed articles called photo essays. Photo essays are stories told by photographs. This new kind of reporting was perfect for Margaret. She went back to Europe during World War II. She and Erskine were the only American reporters in the Soviet Union when the German army attacked.

Margaret became the first female war reporter. She was fearless. She went to places where battles happened. She took important war photos in Italy and Africa. She flew on raids and took pictures from the air. She was with the U.S. Army when it freed people from a concentration camp at the end of the war.

After the war, Margaret kept working. She took pictures in India and Africa. She helped important causes with her photos. People were able to learn a lot from looking at her pictures. Today, we can learn about history by studying her photos. Her work is a lasting gift to people around the world.

NAME: _____ DATE: _____

MARGARET BOURKE-WHITE
(1904–1971)

1. The last paragraph is mainly about:

    a. what Margaret did during college.

    b. what Margaret did during World War II.

    c. what Margaret did during the 1930s.

    d. what Margaret did after the war ended.

2. What does the word **develop** mean in the passage?

    a. to turn an idea into something real

    b. to dig deep into a subject

    c. to print film and make pictures

    d. to wash things in a bathtub

3. Number the following events in the order they happened.

    _____ Margaret was allowed to take pictures in the Soviet Union.

    _____ Margaret took pictures for her college yearbook.

    _____ Margaret traveled to India.

    _____ Margaret became the first female war reporter.

    _____ Margaret helped her father with his film and photos.

4. Answer the following questions.

    How did Margaret become interested in photos?

    _____

    _____

    Who was Erskine Caldwell?

    _____

    What kinds of things did Margaret like to take pictures of?

    _____

    _____

    When did Margaret take photos in the South?

    _____

5. What do you think a photo essay looks like?

    a. It has a lot of photos and short pieces of writing to tell about them.

    b. It has a lot of words describing something and a small photo to show it.

    c. It has some pictures, but most of the essay is a long piece of writing.

    d. none of the above

BONUS

If you could go anywhere to take pictures, where would you go? What kinds of pictures would you take? Write about a trip and the pictures you would take on it.

RACHEL CARSON
(1907–1964)

The scientist looked at all of her research carefully. Farmers had started to use pesticides, like DDT, to kill bugs and moths, protecting their crops. But near the farmland where the chemicals were used, birds and animals were dying. The scientist had to do something, so she wrote a book. The book told about an environment where only a few sick birds still lived. They could not fly or sing. The woods were quiet. The land itself was dying.

The scientist was Rachel Carson, and the book was titled *Silent Spring*. It was published in 1962 and set off a storm of argument about chemicals. The chemical companies that made DDT said that the book was inaccurate. But, Rachel was certain that DDT was **toxic** to living things.

All of her life, Rachel loved the outdoors. She grew up in a country town, and in school, she studied wildlife and the biology of the sea. Then, she went to work as a scientist for the government. She was not paid very much, so she took a second job writing articles about natural history. She was a good writer, and soon, she was in charge of all of the writing done by the U.S. Fish and Wildlife Service.

But, Rachel longed to write her own books. In 1937, she published an article about the sea for a magazine. In 1941, her first book came out. It was called *Under the Sea-Wind*. Her second book, titled *The Sea Around Us*, came out in 1951. In 1955, she published a third book, *The Edge of the Sea*. These books talked about a magical world that most people did not know about at the time—the environment of the sea. Rachel wrote about the amazing animals and plants that lived in the depths of the world's oceans and about life on the seashore. Her books won prizes, and people loved them.

Then, something terrible happened. Rachel found out that she was seriously ill with cancer. At the same time, she began reading reports about DDT. Rachel feared that she did not have a lot of time left to help, and she wanted to keep writing about the sea. But, she felt that, as a scientist, it was more important to keep poisonous chemicals away from crops and animals.

Her book *Silent Spring* became a best seller. Rachel spoke before Congress, asking for new laws to protect the environment. President John F. Kennedy formed a committee to study the problem, and its findings were that Rachel's research was correct. New laws were passed about the use of DDT and the testing of other chemicals.

Rachel died two years later. But, the work that she did is still remembered, and work goes on to try to keep the living world safe from chemicals and other dangers.

American Women Achievers • CD-104255 • © Carson-Dellosa

RACHEL CARSON
(1907–1964)

The scientist looked at all of the facts carefully. Farmers had started to use pesticides, like DDT, to kill bugs and moths. This helped their crops. But near the farmland, birds and animals were dying. The scientist had to do something. So, she wrote a book. The book told about a place where only a few sick birds still lived. They could not fly or sing. The woods were quiet. The land itself was dying.

The scientist was Rachel Carson. The book was called *Silent Spring*. It came out in 1962. It caused a huge storm of argument. The chemical companies that made DDT said that the book was wrong. But, Rachel was sure that DDT was **toxic** to living things.

All of her life, Rachel loved the outdoors. She grew up in a country town. She studied wildlife and the biology of the sea. Then, she went to work as a scientist for the government. She was not paid very much. So, she took a second job. She wrote articles about nature. She was a good writer. Soon, she was in charge of all of the writing done by the U.S. Fish and Wildlife Service.

But, Rachel wanted to write her own books, too. In 1937, she wrote an article about the sea for a magazine. In 1941, her first book came out. It was called *Under the Sea-Wind*. Her second book was called *The Sea Around Us*. It came out in 1951. In 1955, she wrote a third book, called *The Edge of the Sea*. These books talked about a world that most people did not know about at the time. It was the world of the sea. Rachel wrote about the amazing animals and plants that lived in the depths of the water. She wrote about life on the seashore. Her books won prizes. People loved them.

Then, something very bad happened. Rachel found out that she was very ill. She had cancer. At the same time, she started to read reports about DDT. Rachel feared that she did not have a lot of time left to help. She wanted to keep writing about the sea. But, she knew that it was more important to keep the poison of chemicals away from crops and animals.

Her book *Silent Spring* became a best seller. Rachel spoke before Congress. She asked for new laws to save the environment. President John F. Kennedy made a group to study the problem. This group found that Rachel's research was right. New laws were passed about the use of DDT and testing of other chemicals.

Rachel died two years later. But, the work that she did is still remembered. And, work goes on to try to keep the living world safe from chemicals and other dangers.

© Carson-Dellosa • CD-104255 • American Women Achievers

NAME: _____ DATE: _____

RACHEL CARSON
(1907–1964)

1. The first paragraph is mainly about:

   a. the books about the sea that Rachel wrote.

   b. Rachel's childhood in a country town.

   c. the book about the danger of DDT that Rachel wrote.

   d. Rachel's first job for the government.

2. What does the word **toxic** mean in the passage?

   a. at the top of

   b. nourishing

   c. poisonous

   d. quiet, or silent

3. Number the following events in the order they happened.

   _____ Rachel learned to love the outdoors as a child.

   _____ Rachel's book *The Sea Around Us* came out.

   _____ Rachel's book *Silent Spring* became a best seller.

   _____ Rachel was put in charge of all of the writing by the U.S. Fish and Wildlife Service.

   _____ Rachel learned that she had cancer.

4. Answer the following questions.

   What made Rachel stop writing about the sea?

   _____

   _____

   Who made a special group to look into Rachel's research?

   _____

   What did Rachel study in school?

   _____

   How many of Rachel's books does the article talk about?

   _____

5. Why do you think so many people read *Silent Spring*?

   a. Rachel carefully explained the dangers of chemicals.

   b. Rachel's picture of a silent, dying world scared people and made them want to learn more.

   c. Rachel's other books were popular, so people wanted to read this book, too.

   d. all of the above

BONUS

What do you think is the biggest danger to nature now? Write a paragraph about this danger and what can be done to stop it.

VIRGINIA APGAR
(1909–1974)

Virginia Apgar grew up in New Jersey. When she was in high school, she knew that she wanted to be a doctor. Her father was interested in science, but the young girl might have also wanted to work in medicine because one of her brothers died as a child. She finished college in 1929 and entered medical school.

That year, the Great Depression started. Virginia did not have much money for tuition. She took jobs to earn her way through school, even one catching stray cats.

Virginia wanted to be a **surgeon**, but operating on patients was work that was done mostly by men. So, Virginia became a doctor who oversaw the drugs that kept patients asleep during operations. This was a new field, and Virginia became an expert in it. She was asked to teach at Columbia University, becoming the first woman to head a department at the university's famous medical school.

Next, Virginia became interested in the medicine that women took before giving birth. She wanted to know if these drugs harmed babies during delivery. She found that babies were not given close attention during the first few minutes after birth. Virginia believed that the first minute of life was crucial. She invented a scale to judge whether an infant needed help right away.

The scale is called the Apgar score. It checks a baby's breathing, heart rate, skin color, and other signs immediately. That way, doctors know how to best help the baby. Virginia's scoring system is simple, but nobody had ever thought of doing it before. Today, the Apgar score is used around the world. It is used twice: one minute after birth and five minutes after birth, helping hundreds of thousands of babies.

Virginia went on to give other types of aid to children. She became a director for the March of Dimes in 1959. This group helps children with polio and birth defects. Virginia was gifted at raising money and also gave the group medical advice.

Virginia had a long medical career, but she also made time for fun. She loved to fish and attend baseball games. She played the violin and even learned to construct violins herself! But, she is best remembered for her work on behalf of babies and children. This doctor's ideas are still hard at work for children today.

VIRGINIA APGAR
(1909–1974)

Virginia Apgar grew up in New Jersey. When she was in high school, she knew that she wanted to be a doctor. Her father was interested in science. But, she might have also wanted to work in medicine because one of her brothers died as a child. She finished college in 1929. Then, it was time to go to medical school.

That year, the Great Depression started. Virginia did not have much money. She took jobs to earn her way through school. One of her jobs was catching stray cats.

Virginia wanted to be a **surgeon**. But, operating on patients was work that was done mostly by men. So, Virginia became a doctor who gave drugs to patients to keep them asleep during operations. This was a new field. Virginia became an expert. She was asked to teach medicine at Columbia University. She was the first woman to head a department there.

Next, Virginia became interested in the medicine that women took before giving birth. She wanted to know if these drugs hurt babies. She found that babies were not given close attention during the first minutes after birth. Virginia thought that the first minute of life was very important. She invented a scale to judge whether the baby needed help right away.

The scale is called the Apgar score. It checks a baby's breathing, heart rate, skin color, and other signs right away. That way, doctors know how to help the baby best. Virginia's score is simple, but nobody had ever thought of doing it before. Today, the Apgar score is used around the world. It is used twice: one minute after birth and five minutes after birth. It has helped hundreds of thousands of babies.

Virginia went on to give other help to children. She worked for the March of Dimes starting in 1959. This group helps children with polio and other problems. Virginia was good at raising money. She also helped the group as a doctor.

Virginia had a long career in medicine, but she also made time for fun. She loved to fish. She loved baseball. She played the violin. She even learned to make violins herself! But, she is best remembered for her work for babies and children. This doctor's ideas are still hard at work for children today.

NAME: _____ DATE: _____

VIRGINIA APGAR
(1909–1974)

1. This story tells about:

   a. a woman who wanted to become a surgeon.

   b. a doctor who invented a new way to help babies after birth.

   c. a female doctor who worked for the March of Dimes.

   d. all of the above

2. What does the word **surgeon** mean in the passage?

   a. a doctor who takes care of babies

   b. a doctor who tests for cancer

   c. a doctor who operates on patients

   d. a doctor who takes care of teeth

3. Number the following events in the order they happened.

   _____ Virginia finished college in 1929.

   _____ Virginia's brother died.

   _____ Virginia started teaching.

   _____ Virginia invented the Apgar score.

   _____ Virginia entered a new field of medicine after medical school.

4. Answer the following questions.

   What is the Apgar score?
   _____
   _____

   What school hired Virginia to teach in her field?
   _____

   Where did Virginia grow up?
   _____

   What was one of Virginia's hobbies?
   _____

5. What medical field did Virginia go into?

   a. She learned how to deliver babies.

   b. She gave drugs to patients to keep them asleep during operations.

   c. She took care of people with broken bones.

   d. She raised money for people who had cancer.

BONUS

Do you know a doctor or nurse? Write a paragraph about that person. Tell what you know about the kind of work that he or she does.

BABE DIDRIKSON ZAHARIAS
(1911–1956)

She was not a very good student, but when she played a sport—any sport—she was a star. The daughter of immigrants, Mildred "Babe" Didrikson was raised in Texas. Her family was poor, but Babe did not require money to do what she did best. In high school, Babe was the leader of her basketball team. A company, seeing her play, hired her to play on their corporate team. Babe could score 30 points all by herself during games where 20 points was a good score for a whole team! But, Babe pushed herself to do even more.

Next, she switched to track and field. Beginning in 1930, Babe started to set track and field records. She made the Olympic team in 1932 and won two gold medals and a silver medal. Babe also broke three world records during the 1932 Olympic games.

After the Olympics, Babe returned to basketball for a while. She was still a great player, and during the hard times of the 1930s, she made money playing games against men's teams. But, Babe got restless again. She had a new game she wanted to try: golf.

In 1933, Babe started to take golf lessons. Sometimes, she hit a thousand balls a day, staying on the course for hours. Her hands would hurt badly. But, Babe refused to play a sport unless she was the best.

And, she became the best. Babe could drive a golf ball farther than most men. She won 17 **tournaments** in a row in 1943. The next year, Babe helped start a professional tour for female golfers.

Babe met her husband, George Zaharias, in 1938. He was a wrestler, but after they married, George helped Babe with her career by becoming her manager. He was always by her side, cheering on this amazing athlete.

In 1953, after playing golf for 20 years, Babe found out that she had cancer. She did not let the disease stop her. She came back on the professional tour, and she won five tournaments in a row in 1954. She also played games to help raise money for cancer research. Babe fought hard until she died in 1956.

Babe was named Female Athlete of the Year six times during her lifetime by the Associated Press. At a time when women did not participate in many sports, Babe forged paths for women to follow in track and field, basketball, and golf. She is still thought of as the greatest and most versatile female athlete of all time.

BABE DIDRIKSON ZAHARIAS
(1911–1956)

She was not a very good student. But, when she played a sport—any sport—she was a star. The daughter of immigrants, Mildred "Babe" Didrikson was raised in Texas. Her family was poor. But, Babe did not need money to do what she did best. In high school, Babe was the leader of her basketball team. A company hired her to play on their team. Babe could score 30 points all by herself. This was in games where 20 points was a good score for a whole team! But, Babe wanted to do more.

Next, she switched to track and field. In 1930, Babe started to set track and field records. She made the Olympic team in 1932. She won two gold medals and a silver medal. Babe also broke three world records.

After the 1932 Olympics, Babe went back to playing basketball for a while. She was still a great player. During the hard times of the 1930s, she made money playing games against men's teams. But, Babe got restless again. She had a new game she wanted to try. She wanted to play golf.

In 1933, Babe started to take golf lessons. Sometimes, she hit a thousand balls a day. Her hands would hurt a lot. But, Babe would not play a sport unless she was the best.

And, she became the best. Babe could drive a golf ball farther than most men. She won 17 **tournaments** in a row in 1943. The next year, Babe helped start a pro tour for female golfers.

Babe met her husband, George Zaharias, in 1938. He was a wrestler. After they married, George became Babe's manager. He helped Babe with her career. He was always by her side, cheering on this amazing athlete.

In 1953, after playing golf for 20 years, Babe found out that she had cancer. She did not let it stop her. She came back on the pro tour. In 1954, she won five tournaments in a row. She also played games to help raise money for cancer research. Babe fought hard until she died in 1956.

Babe was named Female Athlete of the Year six times during her life by the Associated Press. At a time when women did not play many sports, Babe forged paths for women to follow in track and field, basketball, and golf. She is still thought of as the greatest female athlete of all time.

NAME: _____ DATE: _____

BABE DIDRIKSON ZAHARIAS
(1911–1956)

1. Choose a good title for this story.

    a. No Good at Sports

    b. A Great Female Golfer

    c. The Amazing, All-Around Athlete

    d. Marriage to a Wrestler

2. What does the word **tournaments** mean in the passage?

    a. series of contests or games, each ending with one final round to win

    b. games with two teams playing against each other

    c. sporting events in track and field

    d. events that occur only at the Olympics

3. Number the following events in the order they happened.

    _____ Babe went back to playing basketball after 1932.

    _____ Babe married George Zaharias.

    _____ Babe won 17 golf tournaments in a row.

    _____ Babe made the Olympic team in 1932.

    _____ Babe grew up in Texas.

4. Answer the following questions.

    What was the first sport that Babe played?
    _____

    Who became Babe's manager?
    _____

    What golf event did Babe help start?
    _____

    How many medals did Babe win in the Olympics?
    _____

5. Why is Babe remembered as a pioneer for women's sports?

    a. She created sporting events just for women.

    b. She was a great female golfer.

    c. She played so well that she proved women could compete in the world of sports.

    d. all of the above

BONUS

Imagine that you live at a time when women are discouraged from playing sports. Write a letter telling why women should be able to play any sport that they like.

ROSA PARKS
(1913–2005)

Rosa Parks lived in Alabama and grew up on her grandparents' farm. After going to school, Rosa went to live in the city of Montgomery. She got married and found a job as a seamstress, or a person who sews clothing. Rosa and her husband joined the National Association for the Advancement of Colored People (NAACP) because they wanted to make life better for black people.

But, life for African Americans was hard in Montgomery. Everything for black people was segregated. The bus system was just one example. When black people rode the bus, they had to sit in a section in the back. If a white person demanded the seat of a black person, the black person had to stand up and give away the seat.

On the night of December 1, 1955, Rosa was riding the bus home from work. She was tired from her long day. But more than that, she was tired of being treated as a lesser person. The white section of the bus was full. When a white man told Rosa to give up her seat, Rosa refused to do so.

The bus driver called the police. Rosa was arrested. The next day, a new group was formed in Montgomery to start a **boycott** of the buses. That meant that all black people agreed not to ride the buses until the rules were changed and they were treated the same way as white people. Rosa helped with this boycott. The group was led by Dr. Martin Luther King Jr.

The boycott lasted for more than a year. Meanwhile, Rosa's case went all of the way to the Supreme Court. The Supreme Court ruled that Montgomery's bus laws were wrong. Rosa changed life in Montgomery forever with her simple wish to be treated as an equal.

Rosa worked for civil rights for the rest of her life. In 1965, she went to work as a secretary for U.S. Representative John Conyers, who was also a supporter of civil rights. She retired in 1988.

In 1992, Rosa wrote an autobiography for younger readers called *Rosa Parks: My Story*. The book told about her life up to the bus boycott and told children about the important difference one person can make.

This woman's brave act made life better for all Americans and reminded us that we all can help change the world.

ROSA PARKS
(1913–2005)

Rosa Parks lived in Alabama. She grew up on a farm. The farm was owned by her grandparents. Rosa went to school. Then, she went to live in the city of Montgomery. She got married. She found a job sewing clothing. Rosa and her husband joined the National Association for the Advancement of Colored People (NAACP). They wanted to make life better for black people.

Life for black people in the city was hard. Black people could ride on the buses. But, they had to sit in the back. Sometimes, a white person wanted a black person's seat. The black person had to stand up. He had to give away his seat.

Then came the night of December 1, 1955. Rosa was riding the bus home from work. She was tired from her long day. But, she was also tired of being treated as a lesser person. The white part of the bus was full. A white man told Rosa to give up her seat. Rosa would not stand up.

The bus driver called the police. Rosa was arrested. The next day, a new group was formed in Montgomery. This group started a **boycott** of the buses. This meant that all black people said that they would not ride the buses. They would not pay for bus rides until they were treated the same way as white people. Rosa helped with this boycott. The group was led by Dr. Martin Luther King Jr.

The boycott lasted for more than a year. Rosa's case went all of the way to the Supreme Court. The Supreme Court ruled that Montgomery's bus laws were wrong. Rosa changed life in Montgomery forever with her simple wish to be treated as an equal.

Rosa worked for civil rights for the rest of her life. She went to work as a secretary for U.S. Representative John Conyers in 1965. He was also a supporter of civil rights. Rosa retired in 1988.

In 1992, Rosa wrote an autobiography for younger readers called *Rosa Parks: My Story*. The book told about her life up to the bus boycott. It also told children about the important difference one person can make.

This woman's brave act made life better for all Americans. It also reminded us that we can all make a difference.

NAME: _____ DATE: _____

ROSA PARKS
(1913–2005)

1. The third paragraph is mostly about:

   a. Rosa Parks's childhood.

   b. what Rosa Parks did later in her life.

   c. the night of Rosa Parks's famous bus ride.

   d. how Rosa Parks met Dr. Martin Luther King Jr.

2. What does the word **boycott** mean in the passage?

   a. not buying a service or a thing until a wrong is righted

   b. getting a big group of people to buy or use something to help earn money

   c. drawing or painting designs on something

   d. paying to get something fixed

3. Number the following events in the order they happened.

   _____ Rosa refused to give her seat on the bus to a white man.

   _____ Rosa worked for civil rights for the rest of her life.

   _____ Black people in Montgomery, Alabama, would not ride the buses.

   _____ Dr. Martin Luther King Jr. formed a group to help change the bus laws.

   _____ Rosa Parks got married.

4. Answer the following questions.

   What happened on December 1, 1955?
   _____
   _____

   What was the name of the city where Rosa Parks lived?
   _____

   What did Rosa Parks do for a job?
   _____

   Who ruled that the bus laws were wrong?
   _____

5. How did Rosa's act help all Americans?

   a. It helped make America a more equal, fair society.

   b. Rosa was able to sit where she wanted on the buses in Alabama.

   c. Rosa was a famous part of the civil rights movement.

   d. none of the above

BONUS

When people vote, write letters to newspapers, or go to court, they are using their civil rights. Talk with your classmates. What are other examples of civil rights? Why are they important?

© Carson-Dellosa • CD-104255 • American Women Achievers

EUNICE SHRIVER
(1921– _____)

Eunice Kennedy grew up in a big family. All of her brothers and sisters played sports. They went sailing and loved to play football. Eunice's sister Rosemary took part in these sports, too.

But, Rosemary was not like the other children in the family. She had a hard time reading, and she was not able to learn some things. When Rosemary got older, she had an operation on her brain. It was supposed to help her, but it did not. Eunice felt like she had lost her sister forever.

Eunice wanted to help other children like Rosemary. She married a man named Sargent Shriver. They bought a large farm in Maryland. Starting in 1963, Eunice held a camp there every summer for children who spent most of the year in special schools. They could come to the farm and play outdoors, taking part in kickball games and swimming races. Eunice found that many of these children were good at sports, just like her sister Rosemary.

Eunice decided that she could take this idea even further. She wanted to hold Olympic games for children and adults with special challenges. In 1968, the first Special Olympics event was held in Chicago, Illinois. One thousand people took part in the games, attending from 26 states. The event was a big success.

So, Eunice started an organization to help these athletes train. It also focused on raising money for the games. Eunice found **volunteers** who gave their time to make the Special Olympics happen. She built the organization. She helped with fund-raising. Every year, the Special Olympics grew.

Today, more than one million athletes take part in the Special Olympics. There are games in 150 different countries. Eunice Shriver was awarded the Medal of Freedom for her amazing work and dedication.

The Special Olympics do more than just train athletes. They help the children and adults who take part in the sporting events. Achievement in sports helps them in other parts of their lives, too. And, it shows people that even though these athletes live with challenges, they can do great things.

EUNICE SHRIVER
(1921– _____)

Eunice Kennedy grew up in a big family. All of her brothers and sisters played sports. They went sailing. They loved to play football. Eunice's sister Rosemary did these things, too.

But, Rosemary was not like the other children in the family. She had a hard time reading. She was not able to learn some things. When Rosemary got older, she had surgery on her brain. It was supposed to help her. It did not. Eunice felt like she lost her sister.

Eunice wanted to help other children like Rosemary. She married a man named Sargent Shriver. They bought a big farm in Maryland. Starting in 1963, Eunice held a camp there every summer. It was for children who went to special schools. They could come to the farm and play outside. They played kickball and went swimming. Eunice found that many of these children were good at sports, just like her sister Rosemary.

Eunice thought that she could take this idea even further. She wanted to hold Olympic games for children and adults with special challenges. In 1968, the first Special Olympics event was held. One thousand people took part in the games. They came from 26 states. The event was held in Chicago, Illinois. It was a big success.

So, Eunice started a group. It helped these athletes train. It helped raise money for the games. Eunice found **volunteers**, people who give their time, to make the Special Olympics happen. She built the group. She helped raise money. Every year, the group grew.

Today, more than one million athletes take part in the Special Olympics. There are games in 150 different countries. Eunice Shriver was given the Medal of Freedom for her amazing work.

The Special Olympics do more than just train athletes. They help the children and adults who are part of the sporting events. Doing well in sports helps them in other parts of their lives, too. And, it shows people that even though these athletes live with challenges, they can do great things.

NAME: _____ DATE: _____

EUNICE SHRIVER
(1921– _____)

1. Which word best describes Eunice Shriver?

    a. bored

    b. determined

    c. lazy

    d. quiet

2. What does the word **volunteers** mean in the passage?

    a. people who train to be coaches

    b. people who are paid money for special skills

    c. people who give time and help for free

    d. people who answer an ad for a job

3. Number the following events in the order they happened.

    _____ Eunice started a camp for children with special challenges.

    _____ Eunice married Sargent Shriver.

    _____ Eunice was given the Medal of Freedom.

    _____ The first Special Olympics event was held.

    _____ Rosemary Kennedy had a failed surgery.

4. Answer the following questions.

    Who was Rosemary Kennedy?

    _____
    _____

    Why did Eunice start a camp at her farm?

    _____
    _____

    Where were the first Special Olympics held?

    _____

    How did Eunice keep the Special Olympics going?

    _____
    _____

5. Why do you think sports and the Special Olympics help the athletes who take part?

    a. It shows them that they can do well at something important.

    b. It shows other people that these athletes can do amazing things.

    c. Sports help many people feel more confident.

    d. all of the above

BONUS

Write a paragraph about a time when you played a game or watched a sports event. How did you feel? What did you like best?

MARIA TALLCHIEF
(1925– _____)

Maria Tallchief said that she was "a typical Indian girl" growing up. She loved to be outdoors. She was shy and quiet. She liked to run in the fields with horses. She looked for arrowheads in the grass.

But, Maria's life took a big turn. She is a part of the Osage Nation. The tribe found oil on its land. Maria and her family got money from the oil. They moved from Oklahoma to Los Angeles, California. Maria started to take **ballet** lessons. She loved dance. She loved music.

Soon, Maria studied with a well-known teacher. Her name was Madame Nijinska. Madame Nijinska told Maria to walk, stand, and move like a ballerina, even when she was not dancing. When she slept, Maria was supposed to sleep like a ballerina! Maria understood what this meant. She was giving her life to dance.

Maria went to New York City, New York, in 1942. Then, she went to Europe. She started to dance. The whole world watched. Soon, Maria danced in major parts. George Balanchine saw Maria dance in 1946. He headed a ballet group and created dances for them. He married Maria that same year. Some of his best work was done to show off Maria's amazing talent. One part that George designed for her was the Sugar Plum Fairy in *The Nutcracker*. One writer who saw Maria dance this part said that she was "a creature of magic."

Maria danced in the New York City Ballet until 1960. She danced with the American Ballet Theater until 1965. Then, she and her sister did something new. They started their own ballet group. It was the Chicago City Ballet. Maria worked with the group until 1987.

People thought that Maria's dance style was beautiful. She made hard parts look easy. She said, "A ballerina takes steps that are given to her and makes them her own." She became known around the world. But, Maria never forgot her American Indian roots. She once said that she loved the dances of her own tribe the best. In 1953, the Osage Nation gave her the name "Woman of Two Worlds." It shows that even though Maria is known in the world, she still belongs to her own people.

MARIA TALLCHIEF
(1925– _____)

Maria Tallchief said that she was like many American Indian girls growing up. She loved to be outdoors. She was shy and quiet. She liked to run in the fields with the horses. She looked for arrowheads in the grass.

But, Maria's life took a big turn. She is a part of the Osage Nation. The tribe found oil on its land. Maria and her family got money from the oil. They moved from Oklahoma to Los Angeles, California. Maria started to take **ballet** lessons. She loved dance. She loved music.

Soon, Maria went to study with a well-known teacher. Her name was Madame Nijinska. Madame Nijinska told Maria to walk, stand, and move like a dancer. She was supposed to do this even when she was not dancing. When she slept, Maria must even sleep like a dancer! Maria knew what this meant. She was giving her life to dance.

Maria went to New York City, New York, in 1942. Then, she went to Europe. She started to dance. The whole world watched. Soon, Maria danced in important parts. George Balanchine saw Maria dance in 1946. He headed a dance group. He created new dances for them. He married Maria that same year. Some of his best work was done to show off Maria's amazing gift. One part that George created for Maria was the Sugar Plum Fairy. This is a big part in *The Nutcracker*. A writer who saw Maria dance this part said that she was "a creature of magic."

Maria danced in the New York City Ballet until 1960. She danced with the American Ballet Theater until 1965. Then, she and her sister did something new. They started their own ballet group. It was the Chicago City Ballet. Maria worked with the group until 1987.

People thought that Maria's dance style was beautiful. She made hard parts look easy. She said that a dancer "takes steps that are given to her and makes them her own." Maria became known around the world. But, she never forgot her tribe or her roots. She once said that she loved the dances of her own tribe the best. In 1953, the Osage Nation gave her the name "Woman of Two Worlds." It shows that Maria is known in the world, but still belongs to her own people.

NAME: _____   DATE: _____

MARIA TALLCHIEF
(1925– _____)

1. This story is mostly about:

   a. Maria Tallchief's work with members of her tribe.

   b. how Maria became famous in Europe.

   c. how Maria became a dancer and became known around the world.

   d. how Maria received a new name from her tribe.

2. What does the word **ballet** mean in the passage?

   a. a type of music used for opera

   b. a style of dance based on formal steps and poses

   c. a type of leap done in the middle of a dance

   d. a special dance of an American Indian tribe

3. Number the following events in the order they happened.

   _____ Maria grew up in Oklahoma.

   _____ George Balanchine created parts for Maria to dance.

   _____ Maria danced in the American Ballet Theater group.

   _____ Maria started the Chicago City Ballet.

   _____ Maria took lessons with Madame Nijinska.

4. Answer the following questions.

   Where did Maria's family get the money for her to take dance lessons?

   _____
   _____

   Who was George Balanchine?

   _____
   _____

   Where did Maria and her sister start their own dance group?

   _____

   What was one part that Maria danced?

   _____
   _____

5. Why did Maria's tribe give her a new name?

   a. The new name showed that she was still a part of the tribe but also famous in the outside world.

   b. The new name was meant to honor Maria.

   c. The new name was a way of casting Maria out of her tribe.

   d. a and b

BONUS

Have you ever seen a ballet or a dance on stage? Write a paragraph about how the dancers moved.

© Carson-Dellosa • CD-104255 • American Women Achievers

ALTHEA GIBSON
(1927–2003)

The girl from Harlem, New York, did not set out to be a pioneer, but that is what Althea Gibson became. She was from a poor family. She did not like school and tried to run away from home several times. But then, she started to play paddle tennis at an inner-city center for kids.

Althea was very good at this game. A musician named Buddy Walker saw Althea play and thought that she could compete at regular tennis. He took her to a club for African American tennis players. Althea learned fast. She loved tennis. She had a powerful serve and was fast on her feet.

At that time, African Americans were not allowed to play tennis at clubs for white players. In 1942, Althea won the girls' single title of the American Tennis Association (ATA). She won again in 1944 and 1945. A wealthy person gave Althea help and money so that she could move south. She took tennis lessons and later attended college. Then, she became a tennis teacher. But, she was still blocked from playing in major tennis events.

In 1950, a writer named Alice Marble wrote about Althea. She said that Althea could possibly be the best player in women's tennis, but no one would know for sure until she was allowed to play against all players, black and white. The essay was a challenge. At last, the world of tennis opened up to Althea.

After that, there was no stopping her. Althea was the first African American woman to play at Wimbledon, the famous British tournament. In 1956, she won the French Open. In 1957, she won two events at Wimbledon: the women's singles and the women's doubles.

When she went home to New York City, New York, there was a huge parade in her honor.

Althea still faced **prejudice**. Sometimes, she could not stay at a hotel because she was black. Althea said that she did not care. What she really cared about was her sport, and Althea kept winning tennis games. She won two U.S. Championships and was named Female Athlete of the Year by the Associated Press twice.

But, there was no way for Althea to earn much money at playing tennis. It was not a professional game at the time she played. She went back to teaching after she retired from the sport. Althea wrote a book about her life and even had a part in a movie.

When Althea died, there were many African American tennis players. Arthur Ashe, Serena Williams, and Venus Williams were all able to play tennis because of Althea's pioneering work in the sport. She opened the door for them. Althea led the way.

American Women Achievers • CD-104255 • © Carson-Dellosa

ALTHEA GIBSON
(1927–2003)

The girl from Harlem, New York, did not set out to be a pioneer. But, that is what Althea Gibson became. She was from a poor family. She did not like school. She tried to run away from home. But then, she started to play paddle tennis at a center for city kids.

Althea was very good at this game. A musician named Buddy Walker saw Althea play. He thought that she could play regular tennis. He took her to a club for black tennis players. Althea learned fast. She loved tennis. She had a strong serve. She was fast on her feet.

At that time, black people were not allowed to play tennis at clubs for white players. In 1942, Althea won the girls' single title of the American Tennis Association (ATA). She won again in 1944 and 1945. Althea was given help and money to move south. She took tennis lessons. She went to college. Then, she became a tennis teacher. But, she was still blocked from playing in major tennis events.

In 1950, a writer named Alice Marble wrote about Althea. She said that Althea might be the best player in women's tennis. But, no one would know for sure until Althea could play against all players, black and white. The essay was a challenge. At last, the world of tennis opened up to Althea.

After that, there was no stopping her. Althea was the first black woman to play at Wimbledon, the well-known British tournament. In 1956, she won the French Open. In 1957, she won two events at Wimbledon: the women's singles and the women's doubles. When she went home to New York City, New York, there was a big parade in her honor.

Althea still faced **prejudice**. Sometimes, she could not stay at a hotel because she was black. Althea said that she did not care. What she really cared about was her sport. And, Althea kept winning tennis games. She won two U.S. Championships. She was named Female Athlete of the Year by the Associated Press twice.

But, there was no way for Althea to earn much money at playing tennis. It was not a professional game when she played. She went back to teaching after she stopped playing. Althea wrote a book about her life. She even had a part in a movie.

When Althea died, there were many black tennis players. Arthur Ashe, Serena Williams, and Venus Williams were all able to play tennis because of Althea's work. She opened the door for them in tennis. Althea led the way.

NAME: _____ DATE: _____

ALTHEA GIBSON
(1927–2003)

1. What is the main idea of the second paragraph?

    a. how Althea went south to go to school

    b. how Althea was kept from playing against white players

    c. how Althea began to train to play tennis

    d. how Althea did at Wimbledon

2. What does the word **prejudice** mean in the passage?

    a. openness to people of all races

    b. acceptance of limits

    c. judgment of someone without knowing her, based on the way she looks

    d. the final words of a judge in a trial

3. Number the following events in the order they happened.

    _____ Althea tried to run away from home a few times.

    _____ Althea won the French Open.

    _____ Althea played in the ATA and won tournaments.

    _____ Althea went with Buddy Walker to a tennis club.

    _____ Althea won two events at Wimbledon in 1957.

4. Answer the following questions.

    What was the first sport that Althea played?
    _____

    Who was Alice Marble?
    _____
    _____

    Where did Althea grow up?
    _____

    What job did Althea take after she finished college?
    _____

5. Why was Alice Marble's essay so important to Althea?

    a. Alice Marble's words shamed people into letting Althea play tennis against white players, as well as black players.

    b. Alice Marble said that she would take people to court if Althea could not play in the important tennis matches.

    c. Alice Marble wrote an essay that made people think that Althea was not as good a player as she really was.

    d. none of the above

BONUS

Write a story about a person who really wants to do something—like paint a painting or become a teacher—but is kept from doing it. How would that person feel? How would he or she deal with the unfairness?

SANDRA DAY O'CONNOR
(1930– _____)

Sandra Day O'Connor was the first woman to sit on the Supreme Court, the highest court in the United States. Sandra became a justice of the court in 1980. Before that, she had a difficult time starting her career.

Other people might have given up. But, Sandra was tough. She was raised on the Lazy-B Ranch in Texas, a place without running water and electric lights. The nearest neighbors lived 25 miles away! It was an isolated life. Sandra had pets to keep her from being lonely. She even tamed a bobcat. She also read many books. She learned how to ride horses so that she could help with the ranch work.

Sandra grew up thinking that she would always live and work on the Lazy-B, but her parents had legal troubles with the ranch and had to go to court. Sandra got to see how the law worked and decided that she would study law.

Sandra finished law school when she was only 22 years old. The year was 1952. At that time, no one wanted to give a job to a female lawyer. Sandra searched for a job without success. One law firm said that it would hire her only as a legal secretary.

Finally, Sandra found a job as an attorney for San Mateo County in California. The next year, her husband, John, took a job in Germany. Sandra traveled to Europe with him and worked as a lawyer there.

The O'Connors later came back to the United States and had three sons. Sandra again had a hard time finding a job, so she opened her own law firm in Arizona. She also continued to work for the public, serving in all three branches of the Arizona state government.

It was President Ronald Reagan who asked Sandra if she would serve on the Supreme Court. Sandra worked as a justice until 2005. She always tried to see both sides of each case, even when the court was split in two by an issue. Sandra often had to cast the final vote. She usually tried to help the two sides find a middle ground.

Sandra is now **retired**, but she remains very busy. She gives speeches about how important it is to keep the court system as a separate branch of government. She feels that this part of the United States Constitution must be protected. Sandra also works on projects for a group called the United States Institute of Peace.

Sandra will always be remembered for being the first woman to serve on the U.S. Supreme Court. And, she continues to work for peace and justice around the world.

SANDRA DAY O'CONNOR
(1930– _____)

Sandra Day O'Connor was the first woman to sit on the Supreme Court. The Supreme Court is the highest court in the United States. Sandra became a special judge, called a justice, of the court in 1980. Before that, she had a difficult time starting her career.

Other people might have given up. But, Sandra was tough. She was raised on a ranch in Texas. It was called the Lazy-B Ranch. It did not have running water. It did not have electric lights. The nearest neighbors lived 25 miles away! Sandra had pets to keep her from being lonely. She even had a pet bobcat. She read many books. She learned how to ride horses so that she could help with the ranch work.

Sandra grew up thinking that she would always live on the Lazy-B. But then, her parents had to go to court for their ranch. Sandra got to see how the law worked. That is when she decided that she would study law.

Sandra finished law school when she was only 22 years old. The year was 1952. At that time, no one wanted to give a job to a female lawyer. Sandra looked very hard for a job. One law firm said that it would hire her only as a secretary.

Finally, Sandra found a job. She became a lawyer for San Mateo County in California. The next year, her husband, John, took a job in Germany. Sandra went with him. She worked as a lawyer there, too.

The O'Connors later came back to the United States. They had three sons. Again, she could not find a job. So, she opened her own law firm in Arizona. She also worked for the public. She served in all three branches of the Arizona state government.

It was President Ronald Reagan who asked Sandra if she would serve on the Supreme Court. Sandra worked as a justice until 2005. She always tried to see both sides of each case. Sometimes, the court was split in two by a case. Sandra often had to cast the final vote. She tried to help the two sides find a middle ground.

Sandra is now **retired**. But, she is very busy. She gives speeches about the court system. She talks about how important it is to keep the court system as its own branch of government. She feels that this part of the U.S. Constitution must be protected. Sandra also works on projects for a group called the United States Institute of Peace.

Sandra will always be remembered for being the first woman to serve on the U.S. Supreme Court. And, she continues to work for peace and fairness around the world.

American Women Achievers • CD-104255 • © Carson-Dellosa

NAME: _____ DATE: _____

SANDRA DAY O'CONNOR
(1930– _____)

1. What is the main idea of the second paragraph?

   a. Sandra's husband took a job in Germany.

   b. Sandra could not find a job after she became a lawyer.

   c. Sandra's childhood on a ranch made her tough and independent.

   d. Sandra became the first female justice of the Supreme Court.

2. What does the word **retired** mean in the passage?

   a. quit a job and stopped working full-time

   b. unable to find a job

   c. went to bed

   d. weary

3. Number the following events in the order they happened.

   _____ Sandra graduated from law school.

   _____ Sandra opened her own law firm.

   _____ Sandra served on the Supreme Court as the first female justice.

   _____ Sandra grew up as a cowgirl in Texas.

   _____ Sandra moved to Germany with her husband.

4. Answer the following questions.

   What is the Supreme Court?

   _____

   _____

   What was the Lazy-B?

   _____

   _____

   How long was Sandra a justice of the Supreme Court?

   _____

   Who asked Sandra to take a seat on the Supreme Court?

   _____

5. Why do you think it was so hard for Sandra to find a job as a lawyer?

   a. In 1952, it was against the law for women to be lawyers.

   b. In 1952, people thought that only men could be good lawyers.

   c. In 1952, there were too many female lawyers.

   d. In 1952, Sandra had not finished law school.

BONUS

What would it be like to grow up on a ranch? Write a story about the work on a ranch. Would it be fun? Would it be hard work? Do you think that you would like it?

© Carson-Dellosa • CD-104255 • American Women Achievers

TONI MORRISON
(1931– _____)

Toni Morrison loves stories. As a child, she was always reading books. She was the second of four children born in her Ohio family. She loved to listen to her father tell tales. He told her folktales that he had heard as a child from other African Americans.

Toni went to Howard University. She studied English. She went to Cornell University and got a master's degree. Then, she got a job teaching at a college.

As Toni got older, her life became very busy. She got married and had two children. She got a job as an editor. That means she helped publish other people's books in print. She also kept teaching.

But, the most important thing that Toni did was start writing stories of her own. Her first book came out in 1970. It is about an African American girl who wants to have blue eyes like a movie star. It is set in the Ohio town where Toni grew up. All of Toni's books for grown-ups are about the lives of African Americans in the United States. In a way, Toni's writing carries on the tradition of storytelling that she learned from her father.

Toni's books have won the most important awards that can be given to a writer. Her book *Beloved*, written in 1987, won the Pulitzer Prize. This is an important American award. In 1993, Toni was given the Nobel Prize in Literature. This worldwide prize is given to a writer for her whole **body** of work.

Toni started working on something new in 2002. She started to write books for children. She writes these books with her son, Slade. One of the books, *The Big Box*, is about a group of children who live in a cardboard box. Some of the books, like *Who's Got Game?: The Ant and the Grasshopper*, are based on folktales. Toni and her son make the books fun to read. They have a lot of rhyming words and funny pictures. This is another way that Toni keeps the tradition of telling stories and folktales alive in her family.

TONI MORRISON
(1931– _____)

Toni Morrison loves stories. She was always reading books as a child. She was the second of four children in her Ohio family. She loved to listen to her father tell tales. He told her folktales that he had heard as a child from other black people.

Toni went to Howard University. She studied English. Then, she went to Cornell University. She got a master's degree. She found a job teaching at a college.

As Toni got older, her life was very busy. She got married. She had two children. She got a job as an editor. That means she helped bring out other people's books in print. She also kept teaching.

But, the most important thing that Toni did was start writing stories of her own. Her first book came out in 1970. It is about a young black girl. The girl wants to have blue eyes like a movie star. The book is set in the Ohio town where Toni grew up. All of Toni's books for grown-ups are about the lives of black people in America. In a way, Toni's writing carries on the storytelling that she learned from her father.

Toni's books have won important awards. Her book *Beloved* was written in 1987. It won the Pulitzer Prize. This is a major American award. In 1993, Toni was given a Nobel Prize. This is worldwide prize. The writing prize is given to a writer for her whole **body** of work.

Toni started working on something new in 2002. She started writing books for children. She writes these books with her son, Slade. One of the books, *The Big Box*, is about a group of children who live in a cardboard box. Some of the books, like *Who's Got Game?: The Ant and the Grasshopper*, are based on folktales. Toni and her son make the books fun to read. They have a lot of rhyming words. They have funny pictures. It is another way that Toni keeps the idea of telling stories and folktales alive in her family.

NAME: _____ DATE: _____

TONI MORRISON
(1931– _____)

1. Which of the following best describes Toni Morrison?

   a. sad
   b. creative
   c. quiet
   d. lazy

2. What does the word **body** mean in the passage?

   a. a human's torso, arms, and legs
   b. a whole collection of something
   c. a protest group
   d. a government

3. Number the following events in the order they happened.

   _____ Toni wrote her first book.
   _____ Toni started teaching.
   _____ Toni won the Nobel Prize for her books.
   _____ Toni and Slade Morrison wrote *The Big Box*.
   _____ Toni finished college and got a master's degree.

4. Answer the following questions.

   Where did Toni Morrison grow up?
   _____

   Who told Toni stories and folktales when she was a child?
   _____

   What year did Toni's book *Beloved* come out?
   _____

   Who helps write the children's books that Toni works on today?
   _____

5. How has Toni carried on her father's gift for storytelling?

   a. She writes stories about black people.
   b. She writes children's books based on folktales.
   c. She works on stories with other people in her family.
   d. all of the above

BONUS

Think about a story that someone in your family has told you. Write it down and share it.

RITA MORENO
(1931– _____)

There are four important awards for performers in the United States. One is the Oscar®, for work in movies. One is the Emmy®, for work on TV. One is the Tony®, for work in stage plays. And, the fourth is the Grammy®, for work in music.

There are only three women who have won all four of these impressive awards, and only one Hispanic American woman has done this. That woman is Rita Moreno.

But, Rita's work as an actor, dancer, and singer did not always look **promising**. Rita was born to a family of impoverished farmers in Puerto Rico. She came with her mother to the United States for a better life. Rita was five years old when she came to New York City, New York. Right away, it was evident that Rita had talent for theater work. She danced in a show when she was 7 years old, her first acting part on stage came when she was 13, and she earned a part in her first film when she was only 17 years old.

But for the next 10 years, Rita's parts were not substantial ones. She played Hispanic women, American Indians, and a slave princess in Thailand. She once said that in every part, she was barefoot. Because of her race, she was not given starring parts or challenging roles. This showed prejudice in the way she was selected for her parts.

That changed in 1961 when Rita got a part in *West Side Story*. It was a very important movie, in which Rita played a girl from Puerto Rico. She acted, sang, and danced in her part. The film's story, based on the play *Romeo and Juliet*, presented a strong message against prejudice. Rita won an Oscar® for her role, which placed her work in the spotlight.

Rita continued acting on the Broadway stage. She was given many excellent parts in plays. She also kept working in films. Rita married a doctor named Lenny Gordon in 1965. He helped manage her career.

In the 1970s, Rita tried something new: TV. She starred in a show for children called *The Electric Company*. She won one of her Grammy® Awards for a recording of her singing in this show. She also acted in *The Muppet Show* with the popular Muppets. Rita chose these parts because she had a young daughter. She wanted her daughter and other children to see a Puerto Rican in the shows that they watched and enjoyed. She continues to perform on TV today.

With her work, Rita helps other Hispanic performers. She was able to break away from the small, demeaning parts she got at the start of her career. She has been told by other actors that she shows them what is possible to achieve, regardless of race.

RITA MORENO
(1931– _____)

There are four big awards for performers in the United States. One is the Oscar®, for work in movies. One is the Emmy®, for work on TV. One is the Tony®, for work in stage plays. And, the fourth is the Grammy®, for work in music.

There are only three women who have won all four of these big awards. Only one Hispanic American woman has done this. That woman is Rita Moreno.

But, Rita's work as an actor, dancer, and singer did not always look **promising**. Rita was born to a family of poor farmers. She and her mother came to the United States from Puerto Rico. Rita was five years old when she came to New York City, New York. Right away, it was clear that Rita was good on the stage. She danced in a show when she was 7 years old. Her first acting part on stage came when she was 13. And, Rita was given a part in her first film when she was only 17 years old.

But for the next 10 years, Rita's parts were not good ones. She played Hispanic women, American Indians, and a slave princess in Thailand. She once said that in every part, she was barefoot. Because of her race, she was not given big parts or interesting roles. This showed prejudice in the way she was picked for her parts.

That changed in 1961 when Rita got a part in *West Side Story*. It was a very important movie. Rita played a girl from Puerto Rico. She acted, sang, and danced in the part. The movie's story, based on the play *Romeo and Juliet*, spoke against prejudice. Rita won an Oscar® for her role.

Rita returned to acting on the stage. She was given many good parts in plays. She also kept working in movies. Rita got married in 1965. She married a doctor named Lenny Gordon. He helped manage her career.

In the 1970s, Rita tried something new: TV. She starred in a show for kids called *The Electric Company*. She won one of her Grammy® Awards for a recording of her singing in this show. She also acted in *The Muppet Show* with the Muppets. Rita chose these parts because she had a young daughter. She wanted her daughter and other children to see someone from Puerto Rico in the shows that they watched and liked. She continues to act on TV today.

With her work, Rita helps other Hispanic performers. She broke away from the small, bad parts she got at the start of her work life. She has been told by other actors that she helps show them what is possible.

NAME: _____ DATE: _____

RITA MORENO
(1931– _____)

1. Choose a good title for this story.

    a. How Talent Overcame Prejudice

    b. A Famous Actor

    c. Rita Moreno's Childhood

    d. How Rita Moreno Became a TV Star

2. What does the word **promising** mean in the passage?

    a. making many promises

    b. hopeless

    c. breaking many promises

    d. able to become excellent

3. Number the following events in the order they happened.

    _____ Rita got a part in her first movie.

    _____ Rita won an Oscar® for her part in West Side Story.

    _____ Rita married Dr. Lenny Gordon.

    _____ Rita danced on the stage for the first time.

    _____ Rita won a Grammy® Award for her singing on TV.

BONUS

If you had a choice—to act on TV, in a movie, or on the stage—which would you pick? Why? Write about your choice and your reasons.

---

4. Answer the following questions.

    What four awards did Rita win?

    _____

    _____

    From what country did Rita and her mother come to the United States?

    _____

    What was the name of one of the TV shows in which Rita starred?

    _____

    _____

    What kind of parts did Rita get before acting in *West Side Story*?

    _____

    _____

5. Why was Rita's career important?

    a. She inspired other Hispanic Americans who wanted to act.

    b. She used her talent to get better parts than some people were willing to give her at first.

    c. She showed that Hispanic women are the most talented actors, dancers, and singers.

    d. a and b

© Carson-Dellosa • CD-104255 • American Women Achievers

MADELEINE ALBRIGHT
(1937– _____)

Madeleine Albright was born in Eastern Europe. When she was a child, her family fled to London, England. The German army took over their homeland. Much later in her life, Madeleine found out why her father and mother had to leave so quickly. Their family was Jewish. They kept their religion secret from Madeleine. Many people in Madeleine's family were taken prisoner by the German army and did not survive.

After World War II ended, Madeleine's family went back home. They did not stay long. The Russian army took over the country next. This time, the family left for the United States and moved to Denver, Colorado.

Madeleine's father became a teacher. He also spent a lot of time teaching Madeleine. He talked to her about politics and governments around the world. One of his students was named Condoleezza Rice. Both Madeleine and Condoleezza later became secretaries of state for the United States.

Madeleine became an American citizen in 1957. She got married and had children. She also kept studying. She had to stay in the hospital when she gave birth to twins. She studied Russian to pass the time. When Madeleine left the hospital, she could speak and write in Russian. Madeleine also knew English, French, Czech, Polish, and Serbian. Knowing all of these languages helped her do her work effectively.

Madeleine earned a PhD in public law. She worked for a senator, the United Nations, and the National Security Council. President Bill Clinton asked Congress to make Madeleine the first female secretary of state in 1997. This is a powerful job. Madeleine worked with United States **allies**. She had to make sure that human rights were protected around the world. She also helped make trade agreements for the United States.

During her work as secretary of state, Madeleine felt that it was best to talk to people, not shut them out. She said that even if you have to be tough with someone, it is always better to talk in person.

Madeleine still works to help people around the world. She is a leader in the Council of Women World Leaders. She works to help women around the world become leaders in their countries' governments.

MADELEINE ALBRIGHT
(1937– _____)

Madeleine Albright was born in Eastern Europe. She was a little girl when her family ran away to London, England. The German army took over Madeleine's homeland. Madeleine was grown up before she found out why her father and mother had to leave so quickly. Their family was Jewish. They kept their religion secret from Madeleine. Many of Madeleine's family members were made prisoners in the war and did not survive.

World War II ended. Madeleine's family went home. But, they had to leave again. The Russian army took over the country next. This time, her family went to the United States. They moved to Denver, Colorado.

Madeleine's father became a teacher. He also spent a lot of time teaching Madeleine. They talked about countries and governments around the world. One of his students was named Condoleezza Rice. Both Madeleine and Condoleezza became secretaries of state.

Madeleine became an American in 1957. She got married and had children. She kept studying. She had to stay in the hospital when she had twins. So, she learned Russian to pass the time. Madeleine could speak and write in Russian when she left the hospital. Madeleine also spoke English, French, Czech, Polish, and Serbian. Knowing all of these languages helped her in her work.

Madeleine earned a PhD in public law. She worked for a senator. Then, she worked for the United Nations. After that, she had a job with the National Security Council. President Bill Clinton asked Congress to make Madeleine the first female secretary of state in 1997. This is a powerful job. Madeleine worked with United States **allies**. She had to make sure that human rights were kept safe around the world. She made trade agreements for the United States.

Madeleine always felt that it was best to talk to people, not shut them out. She said that even if you have to be tough with someone, it is always better to talk in person.

Madeleine still works to help people around the world. She is a leader in the Council of Women World Leaders. She works to help women in other countries. She helps them get good jobs as leaders in their countries.

NAME: _____ DATE: _____

MADELEINE ALBRIGHT
(1937– _____)

1. The first paragraph is mainly about:

   a. why Madeleine's family had to leave their homeland during World War II.

   b. why Madeleine's family went to the United States.

   c. how Madeleine learned Russian.

   d. what Madeleine did as secretary of state.

2. What does the word **allies** mean in the passage?

   a. enemies

   b. backstreets

   c. friends

   d. citizens

3. Number the following events in the order they happened.

   _____ Madeleine went to work for a senator.

   _____ Madeleine was named the first female secretary of state.

   _____ Madeleine was born in Eastern Europe.

   _____ Madeleine became an American citizen.

   _____ Madeleine learned to speak and write in Russian.

4. Answer the following questions.

   Why did Madeleine's family move to the United States?

   _____

   _____

   Who asked Congress to make Madeleine secretary of state?

   _____

   What council does Madeleine work for?

   _____

   How did Madeleine learn Russian?

   _____

   _____

5. Which of the following was something Madeleine did as secretary of state?

   a. She helped make new trade agreements for the United States.

   b. She made new laws.

   c. She led the United Nations.

   d. She voted to go to war.

BONUS

If you were secretary of state, you would need to travel to many places. What country would be most important to visit? What would you want to say to that country's leader?

PAT MORA
(1942– _____)

Pat Mora grew up in El Paso, Texas, near the border between Texas and Mexico. Her parents saw that she had a talent for words. When she finished the eighth grade, they gave Pat a typewriter as a gift, but she did not write for years. She wrote little notes to herself with ideas for books and poems. Then, when she neared the age of 40, Pat started to write, and write, and write.

Pat writes many poems. She says that a poet is a healer, a person who builds bridges between people so that they can relate to the same ideas. Pat feels that she plays this part as a Hispanic woman and an American. She writes in English but uses Spanish words throughout her stories and poems to honor her Mexican heritage. She also sets many of her books in the southwestern United States.

One of her best-known children's books is a tall tale about Doña Flor. Doña Flor is so gigantic that she can pick the stars from the sky like flowers. Children use her tortillas for rafts on the river. She is *una amiga*, a friend, to the whole village. One day, the villagers need her to keep them safe from a fierce animal. Doña Flor is brave, so she goes to find the frightening animal—but instead discovers a secret that is not scary at all.

Pat makes writing her wonderful books look easy, but it was not easy for her to get started. She found that it is very hard for a new writer to get her books **published**. It took her eight years to get her first book for children printed. It was turned down 25 times!

What does Pat tell writers about writing? She says that it is important for them to make time for writing and to read as many books as they can. She thinks that rewriting work can help polish it, even if this is not as fun as writing a story the first time. Pat also states that a writer should welcome his ideas like guests into his home, because a writer needs to love his writing in order to write well. Pat says that her favorite book is always the one she is going to write next—that is the book she is most excited about.

One of Pat's favorite things to do is visit schools. She believes in "book joy," the great feeling of reading and learning new things. Reading was always important to her, so she wants students to love reading, too. Pat helped bring a Mexican tradition to the United States. She learned in 1996 that April 30 is the Day of the Child in Mexico. In the United States, Pat linked this day to children's books and reading. Now, libraries and schools in 15 states celebrate this day, thanks to Pat's hard work. Someday, Pat hopes to bring this day of book joy to everyone in the country.

PAT MORA
(1942– _____)

Pat Mora grew up in El Paso, Texas, near the border between Texas and Mexico. Her parents saw that she had a talent for words. When she finished the eighth grade, they gave Pat a typewriter. But, she did not write for years. She kept little notes. These held ideas for books and poems. Then, when she was close to the age of 40, Pat started to write, and write, and write.

Pat writes many poems. She says that a poet is a healer. A poet builds bridges between people so that they can talk about the same ideas. Pat feels that she plays this part as a Hispanic woman and an American. She writes in English. But, she uses Spanish words in her stories and poems to honor her Mexican background. She also sets many of her books in the southwestern United States.

One of her best-known children's books is a tall tale about Doña Flor. Doña Flor is so big that she can pick the stars from the sky like flowers. The children use her tortillas for rafts on the river. She is *una amiga*, a friend, to the whole village. One day, they need her to keep them safe from a wild animal. Doña Flor is brave. She goes to find the scary animal. But instead, she finds a funny secret that is not scary at all.

Pat makes writing her wonderful books look easy. But, it was not easy to get started. She found that it is very hard for a new writer to get books **published**. It took her eight years to get her first book for children printed. It was turned down 25 times!

What does Pat tell writers about writing? She says that it is important for them to make time for writing. It is also important for them to read as many books as they can. She thinks that rewriting work can make it better, even if it is not as fun as writing a story the first time. Pat also believes that a writer should welcome his ideas like guests into his home. A writer needs to love his writing to write well. Pat says that her favorite book is always the one she is going to write next. It is the book she is most excited about.

One of Pat's favorite things to do is visit schools. She believes in "book joy," the great feeling of reading and learning new things. Reading was always important to her. She wants students to love reading, too. Pat helped bring a Mexican tradition to the United States. April 30 is the Day of the Child in Mexico. Pat learned about this in 1996. She linked this day to children's books and reading. Libraries and schools in 15 states now celebrate this day, thanks to Pat's hard work. Someday, Pat hopes to bring this day of book joy to everyone in the country.

NAME: _____ DATE: _____

PAT MORA
(1942– _____)

1. Choose a good title for this story.

   a. The Woman Who Bridges Two Worlds

   b. Writing for Adults

   c. The Day of the Child

   d. Growing Up on the Border

2. What does the word **published** mean in the passage?

   a. got a book put into the library

   b. wrote a book

   c. printed a book and sold it in stores

   d. drew pictures for a book

3. Number the following events in the order they happened.

   _____ Pat started to write poems.

   _____ Pat learned about the Day of the Child in Mexico.

   _____ Pat's parents gave her a typewriter.

   _____ Pat's first children's book came out.

   _____ Pat brought the Day of the Child to 15 U.S. states.

4. Answer the following questions.

   What does Pat feel that poets do?

   _____

   _____

   How many years did it take Pat to get her first children's book printed?

   _____

   What is the name of Pat's character in her tall tale?

   _____

   Where did Pat grow up?

   _____

5. How does Pat bridge her Hispanic and American backgrounds?

   a. She sets her books in the southwestern United States.

   b. She brought a Mexican tradition to the United States.

   c. She uses Spanish words in her stories.

   d. all of the above

BONUS

Do you know any words in another language? (If you do not know any words in a different language, ask your teacher to help you learn some.) Use the words in a story.

© Carson-Dellosa • CD-104255 • American Women Achievers

ISABEL ALLENDE
(1942– _____)

Isabel Allende was born in Chile, but she spent part of her childhood in other parts of the world. Her stepfather was a diplomat, a person who works with other governments. For a time, Isabel went to school in the Middle East.

When she grew up, Isabel lived in Belgium and worked for the United Nations. Then, she went home to Chile. She had a job as a writer for a children's magazine. She also helped write TV shows. But in 1973, something terrible occurred. The government of Chile was overthrown, and the president was killed. The president was Isabel's uncle.

Her family was in danger and knew that they had to leave the country. This broke Isabel's heart. She had to leave behind some people in her family, including her grandfather. He was 93 years old when she left.

Isabel started to write a letter to her grandfather. She wanted him to know that she would never forget him. She would never forget the stories he told her about their family. Her letter grew longer and longer. Finally, Isabel realized that she was writing a **novel**. She named it *The House of the Spirits*. It came out when she was 40 years old.

Isabel has written many books that are now read around the world. Most of the books are for adults, but in 2002, Isabel completed her first children's novel. The book is about a young boy named Alexander Cold. He takes a trip down the Amazon River, meets a strange tribe called the People of the Mists, and learns their secrets. The book is titled *The City of Beasts*. Isabel has also written two other novels about Alexander's adventures.

Today, Isabel lives in California. She became an American citizen in 2003. She says that she did not feel like an American until the sad day of September 11, 2001. For her, it felt like a tie to the sad times she lived through in Chile. But, she says that in many ways, the United States is foreign to her. She says that people here always feel like they can start over. They can move and start a new life. Even though Isabel has moved many times, she still feels linked to Chile. She still writes about her homeland. She says that she cannot leave her past behind, and she does not want to.

Isabel continues to write many different types of books and articles for adults and children. Her magical, descriptive language helps bring her stories to life for readers. Through her writing, she hopes to bridge the divisions between different cultures.

ISABEL ALLENDE
(1942– _____)

Isabel Allende was born in Chile. But, she spent part of her childhood in other parts of the world. Her stepfather worked with other governments. For a time, Isabel went to school in the Middle East.

When she grew up, Isabel lived in Belgium. She worked for the United Nations. Then, she went home to Chile. She had a job as a writer for a children's magazine. She also helped write TV shows. But in 1973, something bad happened. The government of Chile was taken over. The president was killed. He was Isabel's uncle.

She and her family were in danger. They had to leave the country. This broke Isabel's heart. She had to leave behind some people in her family. One of them was her grandfather. He was 93 years old when she left.

Isabel started to write a letter to her grandfather. She wanted him to know that she would never forget him. She would never forget the stories he told her. Her letter grew longer and longer. Isabel saw one day that she was writing a **novel**. She named it *The House of the Spirits*. It came out when she was 40 years old.

Isabel has written many books. They are now read around the world. Most of the books are for grown-ups. But in 2002, Isabel wrote her first children's book. The book is about a young boy named Alexander Cold. He takes a trip down the Amazon River. He meets a strange tribe called the People of the Mists. He learns their secrets. The book is called *The City of Beasts*. Isabel has also written two other books about Alexander's adventures.

Today, Isabel lives in California. She became an American in 2003. She says that she did not really feel like she could be an American until the sad day of September 11, 2001. For her, it felt like a tie to the sad times she lived through in Chile. But, she says that in many ways, the United States is strange to her. She says that people here always feel like they can start over. They can move and start a new life. Isabel has moved many times. But, she still feels tied to Chile. She still writes about her homeland. She says that she cannot leave her past behind. And, she does not want to.

Isabel still writes many different types of books and articles for adults and children. Her magical, descriptive words help bring her stories to life for readers. Through her writing, she hopes to bridge the gaps between different cultures.

NAME: _____ DATE: _____

ISABEL ALLENDE
(1942– _____)

1. This story tells about:

   a. a woman whose loss of her home led her to write many books.

   b. a writer who likes to tell stories about life on other planets.

   c. a woman whose uncle was killed and who ran for office after his death.

   d. a woman who had to run away from the United States because she was in danger.

2. What does the word **novel** mean in the passage?

   a. something new

   b. something unusual or strange

   c. a short piece of writing that rhymes

   d. a long story with chapters

3. Number the following events in the order they happened.

   _____ Isabel worked as a writer for a children's magazine.

   _____ Isabel wrote *The House of the Spirits*.

   _____ Isabel's uncle was killed.

   _____ Isabel wrote *The City of Beasts*.

   _____ Isabel went to school in the Middle East.

4. Answer the following questions.

   What did Isabel do when she lived in Belgium?

   _____

   _____

   To whom did Isabel start writing a long letter after she left Chile?

   _____

   _____

   When did Isabel become an American citizen?

   _____

   Why did Isabel and her family leave Chile?

   _____

   _____

5. Why do you think Isabel started to write the letter to her grandfather?

   a. She wanted to feel close to him, even though she was in a different country.

   b. He liked to get very long letters.

   c. She knew right away that she was writing a novel.

   d. none of the above

BONUS

If you had to leave your homeland, what do you think it would be like to go to a new country? What would you find hardest to leave behind? Write a story about it.

ANTONIA NOVELLO
(1944– _____)

If Antonia Novello had been healthy as a child, she might not have become a doctor. But, Antonia was born with a serious condition of the colon. She spent at least two weeks every year in the hospital, and the doctors became her friends. Finally, when she was 18, she learned that she could have an operation to fix her problem. After her surgery, however, she had complications that lasted for two years.

During this time, Antonia went to school. Her mother did not give her another choice. Her mother was a principal and made sure that Antonia always had the best teachers and the best opportunities. Even when Antonia was not feeling well, she had to do her best.

When Antonia was 20 years old, she went from her home in Puerto Rico to the Mayo Clinic, a famous hospital in the United States. She had another operation there. This time, Antonia was well when she left the hospital. She said that she did not want anyone else to **suffer** as she had for so many years. After her last operation, she earned her bachelor's degree. She started medical school in 1970.

When she was a doctor, Antonia got a job working for the government. She tried being a children's doctor, but she was too emotional about her patients. She once said that she cried as much as the parents did! So instead, she got a job doing research. She researched AIDS, studying the disease in children. She also worked with members of Congress, helping them obtain information about illnesses when they drafted laws about medicine and health care.

In 1990, Antonia was called to the office of the secretary of health. He asked Antonia if she knew why she was in his office. She thought that he had called her in to look at budgets and the way she handled money for her work. But, he told Antonia that President George H. W. Bush wanted her to be the next surgeon general.

The surgeon general is the most important doctor in the country. Antonia was the first woman to ever hold this job. She was also the first Hispanic American to hold this job. During her time in office, Antonia worked on several important medical issues, most of them involving children. She worked to get shots for all children starting school. She campaigned to help students understand why they should not smoke. Today, she works for the state of New York. She still helps people and teaches about health and better medicine.

ANTONIA NOVELLO
(1944– _____)

If Antonia Novello had been healthy as a child, she might not have become a doctor. But, Antonia was born with a colon problem. She spent at least two weeks every year in the hospital. The doctors became her friends. Then, she learned that she could have an operation to fix her problem. She was 18. After her surgery, she had more problems. These lasted for two more years.

During this time, Antonia went to school. Her mother did not give her another choice. Her mother was a principal. She made sure that Antonia had the best teachers. Even when she was not feeling well, she had to do her best.

When Antonia was 20 years old, she went from her home in Puerto Rico to the Mayo Clinic. This is a well-known hospital in the United States. Antonia had another surgery. This time, she was well when she left the hospital. She said that she did not want anyone else to **suffer** as she had for so many years. She got her bachelor's degree after her last surgery. She started medical school in 1970.

Then, Antonia got a job working for the government. She tried being a children's doctor. But, she was too sad for her patients. She once said that she cried as much as the parents did! So, she got a job doing research. One of the things she researched was AIDS. She studied the disease in children. She also worked with members of Congress. She helped them get information about illnesses when they wrote laws about medicine.

In 1990, Antonia was called to the office of the secretary of health. He asked Antonia if she knew why she was in his office. She thought that he had called her in to look at budgets and the way she handled money for her work. But, he told Antonia that President George H. W. Bush wanted her to be the next surgeon general.

The surgeon general is the top doctor in the country. Antonia was the first woman to hold this important job. She was also the first Hispanic American to hold this job. During her time in office, Antonia worked on several important issues. Many of them involved children. She worked to get shots for all children starting school. She worked to help students understand why they should not smoke. Today, she works for the state of New York. She still helps people and teaches about health and better medicine.

NAME: _____ DATE: _____

ANTONIA NOVELLO
(1944- _____)

1. What is the main idea of this story?

   a. how Antonia Novello was raised by her mother

   b. how Antonia Novello overcame illness to become a doctor and surgeon general

   c. how Antonia Novello went into government because she could not be a doctor

   d. how Antonia Novello works for the state of New York today

2. What does the word **suffer** mean in the passage?

   a. to feel full of energy

   b. to feel pain

   c. to cut something in two

   d. to be very smart

3. Number the following events in the order they happened.

   _____ Antonia went to school even though she was ill.

   _____ Antonia worked as surgeon general to get shots for all students.

   _____ Antonia was called to the office of the secretary of health.

   _____ Antonia went to the Mayo Clinic.

   _____ Antonia finished medical school.

4. Answer the following questions.

   Where was Antonia's home as a child?
   _____

   Who made sure that Antonia had the best teachers?
   _____

   In what year was Antonia asked to become surgeon general?
   _____

   How did Antonia help members of Congress?
   _____
   _____

5. Why do you think Antonia's illness as a child made her want to be a doctor?

   a. She spent time in the hospital and got to know doctors and nurses.

   b. She did not want other people to be as ill as she was.

   c. She was not as ill as the doctors thought she was.

   d. a and b

BONUS

Would you like to be a doctor? Why or why not? Write a paragraph about your choice.
_____

SUE HENDRICKSON
(1949– _____)

Sue Hendrickson loved two activities as a child. She loved to read, and she loved to dig. She always looked for buried treasure. One time, she dug up a tiny brass bottle. Other times, she strolled slowly along sidewalks, looking at the ground and hoping to find interesting things.

It is not a surprise that she grew up to be an explorer who has been on many adventures. Sue taught herself how to dive so that she could collect tropical fish and sell them to pet stores. After one dive, she went hiking with some friends and they visited an amber mine. One piece of amber had an insect trapped inside of it, and a miner told Sue that it was 23 million years old. At that moment, Sue knew that she wanted to search for **fossils**.

Where did she start? She dug up whale bones—in the desert! She worked with a group of archaeologists who looked for the bones of water animals in what used to be a sea. Now, the region is the desert of Peru. Sue helped discover the bones of whales, dolphins, and seals that were hundreds of miles from water.

In 1990, she journeyed to South Dakota. A team of scientists was digging for dinosaur bones. It was on this hot prairie that Sue made a fascinating discovery. The team's truck had a flat tire, and the others went to get the tire fixed. Sue and her dog stayed behind and went for a walk. She wanted to examine some cliffs that they had not had time to explore yet.

Sue saw some bones on the ground and looked up. There in the sandstone cliff was a huge dinosaur skeleton! The group elected to work on Sue's find. They uncovered the biggest, most complete skeleton of a *Tyrannosaurus rex* that has ever been found. Because they were embedded in rock, the bones were preserved. The *T. rex* was named "Sue" after its discoverer.

This was far from Sue Hendrickson's only adventure. Two years later, she dove with scientists to explore a sunken ship. It was a Spanish trading ship. In 1600, it was engaged in a battle and was sunk. At the wreck, scientists found huge stone jars, 100 skeletons, and more than 400 gold and silver coins.

Sue has been on other dives to sunken ships and even to a sunken building! She has plans for more adventures, too. She wants to look for more dinosaurs and hopes to discover a woolly mammoth skeleton. Often, Sue travels to the Field Museum in Chicago, Illinois, her hometown. That is where Sue the *T. rex* is now, on display. Sue the explorer likes to visit Sue the dinosaur whenever she can.

SUE HENDRICKSON
(1949– _____)

Sue Hendrickson loved two things as a child. She loved to read. And, she loved to dig. She always looked for treasure. One time, she dug up a little brass bottle. Other times, she walked along, looking at the ground and hoping to find interesting things.

It's not a surprise that she grew up to be an explorer. Sue has been on many adventures. She taught herself how to dive so that she could collect fish and sell them to pet stores. After one dive, she went hiking with some friends. They saw amber being mined. One piece had a bug trapped inside of it. A miner told Sue that it was 23 million years old. Sue knew then that she wanted to look for **fossils**.

Where did she start? She dug up whale bones—in the desert! She worked with scientists who looked for the bones of water animals in what used to be a sea. Now, it is the desert of Peru. Sue helped find the bones of whales, dolphins, and seals that were hundreds of miles from water.

In 1990, she went to South Dakota. A group of scientists was digging for dinosaur bones. It was there that Sue made a big discovery. The team's truck had a flat tire. The others went to get the tire fixed. Sue and her dog went for a walk. She wanted to look at some cliffs that they had not had time to explore yet.

Sue saw some bones on the ground. She looked up. There in the cliff was a huge dinosaur skeleton! The group worked on Sue's find. They uncovered the biggest, most complete *Tyrannosaurus rex* skeleton that has ever been found. Because they were in rock, the bones were protected. The *T. rex* was named "Sue" after its discoverer.

This was far from Sue Hendrickson's only adventure. Two years later, she dove with scientists to explore a sunken ship. It was a Spanish trading ship. In 1600, it was in a battle and sank. The scientists found huge stone jars. They found 100 skeletons. And, they found more than 400 gold and silver coins.

Sue has been on other dives and found sunken ships and even a sunken building! She has plans for even more adventures. She wants to look for more dinosaurs. She hopes to find a woolly mammoth skeleton. Sometimes, she travels to the Field Museum in Chicago, Illinois. The museum is in her hometown. That is where Sue the *T. rex* is now. There, Sue the explorer visits Sue the dinosaur whenever she can.

NAME: _____ DATE: _____

SUE HENDRICKSON
(1949– _____)

1. Which of the following best describes Sue Hendrickson?

   a. stern

   b. adventurous

   c. quiet

   d. funny

2. What does the word **fossils** mean in the passage?

   a. traces of ancient animals or plants found in the earth's crust

   b. something metal that rusted

   c. a type of watch

   d. one kind of dinosaur

3. Number the following events in the order they happened.

   _____ Sue was born in Chicago, Illinois.

   _____ Sue found a *T. rex* skeleton in South Dakota.

   _____ Sue dove to explore a Spanish treasure ship.

   _____ Sue went to the desert of Peru on a dig.

   _____ Sue wants to look for a woolly mammoth skeleton.

4. Answer the following questions.

   Why did Sue learn how to dive?

   _____
   _____

   Where did Sue go to dig up whale, dolphin, and seal bones?

   _____

   In what year did Sue discover the *T. rex* skeleton?

   _____

   How did the Spanish ship that Sue explored sink?

   _____
   _____

5. How did Sue find the *T. rex* bones?

   a. She was digging in the earth with scientists when they all found the skeleton.

   b. Her dog found the bones and ran back to get her.

   c. She went for a walk while she was waiting for a flat tire to be fixed.

   d. She dove into the ocean, looking for a sunken ship.

BONUS

Write a poem about finding a lost city under the sea. What does it look like? How do you feel?

_____

SALLY RIDE
(1951– _____)

If you had asked the young Sally Ride what she wanted to be when she grew up, she would have said, "A tennis star!" Sally started to play tennis when she was 10 years old. She won many matches and even won a **scholarship** that gave her enough money to attend a private school. Sally started college but left when she decided that she would rather be a professional tennis player. She quickly found out that it was not for her, though. Sally returned to college and studied science.

Sally was 27 years old when she finished college. One day, she saw a newspaper story that said that the National Aeronautics and Space Administration (NASA) was interviewing new astronauts. That was a job that Sally wanted to have! Eight thousand people wrote letters asking for places in the new program. Sally had to attend many interviews and take many tests. At last, NASA made its choices. Only six women were selected. Sally was one of them.

That was only the start of Sally's hard work. She had to learn how to jump out of an airplane, use a radio in space, fly an airplane, and use the equipment on space shuttles. Sally liked flying the best; in fact, it became her favorite hobby.

After five long years of work, Sally got her chance to fly in space. In 1983, she was assigned to the crew of a space shuttle. She was the first American woman in space. She was the communications officer who sent radio messages to Earth and to the crews. She also helped create the mechanical arm that the crew used to send out satellites and pull them back to the shuttle.

In 1984, Sally flew in a space shuttle again. She was preparing to fly in 1986 when the *Challenger* space shuttle failed. Sally was asked to examine the event and helped write a report about the tragic accident.

Sally left NASA in 1987. She became a teacher and still works hard to encourage young women and girls to learn more about science and math. She started a special club, the Sally Ride Science Club, to help make this possible. Sally also led a project at NASA that let students take photos of Earth from space.

Another thing that Sally does is write books for children. Her books are titled *To Space and Back*, *Voyager*, *The Third Planet*, *The Mystery of Mars*, and *Exploring Our Solar System*. Sally Ride started out being excited about tennis. Now, she loves the stars and planets. She wants others to know more about space, flight, and exploring, too.

SALLY RIDE
(1951– _____)

If you had asked the young Sally Ride what she wanted to be when she grew up, she would have said, "A tennis star!" Sally started to play tennis when she was 10 years old. She won many matches. She even won a **scholarship**. This gave her money to go to a private school. Sally started college but left when she thought that she could be a professional tennis player. She quickly found out that it was not for her, though. Sally went back to school. She studied science.

Sally was 27 years old when she finished school. One day, she saw a newspaper story. It said that the National Aeronautics and Space Administration (NASA) wanted new astronauts. That was a job that Sally wanted! Eight thousand people asked for places in the new program. Sally had to go to many interviews. She had to take many tests. At last, NASA made its choices. Only six women were picked. Sally was one of them.

That was only the start of Sally's hard work. She had to learn how to jump out of an airplane. She had to learn how to use a radio in space. She had to learn how to fly an airplane. She learned how to use the equipment on a space shuttle. Sally liked flying the best. It became her favorite hobby.

After five long years of work, Sally got her chance to fly in space. In 1983, she was added to a space shuttle crew. She was the first American woman in space. She was the person who sent radio messages to Earth and to the crews. She also helped create the arm that the crew used to send out satellites and pull them back to the shuttle.

In 1984, Sally flew in a space shuttle again. She was getting ready to fly again in 1986. Then, the *Challenger* space shuttle failed. Sally was asked to study the event. She helped write a report about the sad accident.

Sally left NASA in 1987. She became a teacher. She still works hard to get young women and girls to learn more about science and math. She started a special club, the Sally Ride Science Club, to help make this happen. Sally also led a project at NASA that let students take photos of Earth from space.

Another thing that Sally does is write books for children. Her books are titled *To Space and Back*, *Voyager*, *The Third Planet*, *The Mystery of Mars*, and *Exploring Our Solar System*. Sally Ride started out being excited about tennis. Now, she loves the stars and planets. And, she wants others to know more about space, flight, and exploring.

NAME: _____ DATE: _____

SALLY RIDE
(1951– _____)

1. What is the main idea of the second paragraph?

   a. Sally decided to be a professional tennis player.

   b. Sally found out about a new program at NASA and asked for a job.

   c. Sally was added to a space shuttle crew after long years of training.

   d. Sally became an author.

2. What does the word **scholarship** mean in the passage?

   a. the study of books and ideas

   b. to be very gifted at learning

   c. a gift of money to pay for schooling

   d. the study of outer space

3. Number the following events in the order they happened.

   _____ Sally was asked to study the *Challenger* accident.

   _____ Sally learned how to fly a plane and to use a radio in space.

   _____ Sally became the first American woman in space.

   _____ Sally started playing tennis.

   _____ Sally finished college and read about the astronaut program.

4. Answer the following questions.

   Why did Sally quit college?

   _____
   _____

   How many people asked for places in NASA's astronaut program?

   _____

   In what year did Sally first go into space?

   _____

   How does Sally help young people today?

   _____
   _____

5. Why do you think Sally wants girls to be interested in science and math?

   a. She was, and she had a great career because of it.

   b. She feels that girls should be drawn to science and math as much as boys are.

   c. She wants girls to have chances at interesting jobs like hers.

   d. all of the above

BONUS

Imagine blasting off into space! Write a story about being an astronaut and going into space for the first time. How do you feel? What is your first day in space like?

_____

© Carson-Dellosa • CD-104255 • American Women Achievers

OPRAH WINFREY
(1954– _____)

Oprah Winfrey overcame a hard childhood to get a job in TV. She lived with her grandmother when she was small. Then, she moved in with her mother. She was so unhappy that she ran away when she was 13 years old. The police found her and sent her to live with her father in Nashville, Tennessee. He was strict, making sure she was home early every night. He made her read one book every week and write a report for him about it. That is how Oprah's love of books began.

Oprah's first job in TV was as a **reporter** in Nashville, but she was not very good at reporting the news. Reporters are supposed to be calm and detached from what they talk about. Oprah cried if a story was sad and laughed at funny stories. So, she was given a job hosting a talk show. She was in charge of asking guests questions and running the show. It was shown in Baltimore, Maryland. Then, she went to Chicago, Illinois, to do a show.

Oprah has acted in some movies, but hosting a talk show is her favorite occupation. Oprah's show was broadcast around the United States in 1986, and people loved it. Oprah likes to talk to everybody, and she is easy to talk to. She gives her opinion about things. Her talk show has won many awards.

In 1996, she announced the beginning of Oprah's Book Club. Thousands of people read the books Oprah talks about on her show and share their thoughts on her Web site. Because of Oprah's Book Club, reading has become more popular than ever!

Oprah has become very wealthy. She was the first African American woman to become a billionaire. She gives away a lot of her money to help other people. Oprah gives money to students and to help people in Africa. She started a school for girls in South Africa and has many other projects to help women, students, and poor people. Oprah has an amazing life. One reason for her success is that she treats everyone like a friend.

OPRAH WINFREY
(1954– _____)

Oprah Winfrey overcame a hard childhood to get a job in TV. She lived with her grandmother when she was small. Then, she moved in with her mother. She was so unhappy that she ran away when she was 13 years old. The police found her. They sent her to live with her father in Nashville, Tennessee. He was strict. He made sure she was home early every night. He made her read one book every week. She had to write a report about each book. That is how her love of books started.

Oprah's first job in TV was as a **reporter** in Nashville. She was not very good at reporting the news. Reporters are supposed to be calm. Oprah cried if a story was sad. She laughed at funny stories. So, she was given a job hosting a talk show. She ran the show and asked the guests questions. It was shown in Baltimore, Maryland. Then, she went to Chicago, Illinois, to do a show.

Oprah has acted in some movies. But, hosting a talk show is her favorite thing to do. Oprah's show was broadcast around the United States in 1986. People loved it. Oprah likes to talk to everybody. She tells people what she thinks about things. Her talk show has won many awards.

In 1996, she started Oprah's Book Club. Thousands of people read the books Oprah picks for her book club. Readers can share their thoughts about each book on her Web site. Because of Oprah's Book Club, reading is more popular than ever!

Oprah became very rich. She was the first black woman to become a billionaire. She gives away a lot of money to help other people. Oprah gives money to students. She gives money to help people in Africa. She started a school for girls in South Africa. She has many projects to help women, students, and poor people. Oprah has an amazing life. One reason for this is that she treats everyone like a friend.

NAME: _____ DATE: _____

OPRAH WINFREY
(1954– _____)

1. The last paragraph of this story is mostly about:

   a. how Oprah grew up.

   b. how Oprah helps other people with her money.

   c. how Oprah started working in TV.

   d. how Oprah became an actor.

2. What does the word **reporter** mean in the passage?

   a. a written paper about a book or an event

   b. something that tapes sound

   c. a person who has guests on a TV show where people talk to each other

   d. a person who speaks about news events on TV or the radio

3. Number the following events in the order they happened.

   _____ Oprah went to live with her father.

   _____ Oprah won awards for her show.

   _____ Oprah went to Chicago, Illinois, to host a TV show.

   _____ Oprah lived with her grandmother.

   _____ Oprah left her job as a reporter in Nashville.

4. Answer the following questions.

   Why wasn't Oprah a good news reporter?

   _____

   _____

   In what city did Oprah live with her father?

   _____

   When did Oprah's TV show start showing around the United States?

   _____

   How has Oprah helped young girls in South Africa?

   _____

   _____

5. Why do you think living with her father helped Oprah?

   a. He was strict, but he made her study and took care of her.

   b. He was fun and took her out at night to parties.

   c. He was so strict that she ran away to live with her mother.

   d. He was a good listener, and they grew very close.

BONUS

If you had a TV show with guests, whom would you want to have on your show? Write down the person's name. Then, write a list of five questions you would ask your guest.

NANCY LOPEZ
(1957– _____)

Nancy Lopez played golf with all of her heart and was always cheerful, a fact that made an enormous difference to her fans. When Nancy was 15 years old, she saw a professional golfer be rude to a fan by turning him away when he asked for an autograph. Nancy thought to herself that she would never act like that. Other golfers and her fans loved her for it.

Nancy started playing golf with her father when she was 8 years old and received a set of golf clubs as a gift. The next year, she won a children's tournament in New Mexico, her home state. When she was 12 years old, she won a state championship. Nancy made golf look easy, but it was not easy for Nancy to practice her sport. She is a Hispanic American. Because of that, she was not allowed to play at a nearby golf course. Instead, she and her parents had to drive 200 miles to a course where Hispanic Americans could play. It was a dry, dusty course with dead grass in many places, but it was the best course open to them.

Nancy also faced difficulties in golf because she is a woman. Some courses would not let women play until late in the day. In high school, there was no girls' golf team, so Nancy had to petition to join the boys' team instead. She helped them win the state championship.

Her father aided Nancy in many ways with her ambitions. He taught her what he knew about golf and gave her **tips** about the game. He dug a big pit in their backyard and filled it with sand so that Nancy could use it to learn how to hit balls out of sand traps.

When Nancy started to play professional golf, many people complained. They said that she was too focused on her game, and they did not like the way she played. The truth was that they did not like to see a Hispanic American woman win so many games. Nancy just ignored the prejudice like she always had. She concentrated and worked hard. In 1977, she played in six professional events. Her first full year as a professional golfer was 1978, and she won nine tournaments, including five tournaments in a row. No female golfer has ever beaten her record.

By the time Nancy was 30, she had won 35 tournaments. In 1989, she was added to the Ladies Professional Golf Association (LPGA) Hall of Fame, becoming the youngest woman to have that honor.

Nancy set a goal for herself. She wanted to win 50 tournaments before she retired, and she almost reached that goal. She retired from full-time play in 2002 after winning 48 times, because she knew that it was the right time to retire. She had injured her knees. She had three children and wanted to spend more time with her family. Nancy left golf, but golfers will never forget the amazing career of Nancy Lopez.

NANCY LOPEZ
(1957– _____)

Nancy Lopez played golf with all of her heart. She always seemed happy. It made a big difference to her fans. When Nancy was 15 years old, she saw a professional golfer be rude to a fan. Nancy thought to herself that she would never act like that. Other golfers and her fans loved her for it.

Nancy started playing golf with her father when she was 8 years old. She got a set of golf clubs as a gift. The next year, she won a children's tournament in New Mexico, her home state. When she was 12, she won a state championship! Nancy made golf look easy. But, it was not easy for Nancy to practice. She is a Hispanic American. Because of that, she was not allowed to play at a nearby golf course. Instead, she and her parents had to drive 200 miles to a course where they could play. It was a dry, dusty course. In many places, there was dead grass. But, it was the best course that was open to them.

Nancy also had problems in golf because she is a woman. Some courses would not let women play until late in the day. In high school, there was no girls' golf team. Nancy had to play on the boys' team. She helped them win the state championship.

Her father helped Nancy in many ways. He taught her what he knew about golf. He gave her **tips** about the game. He dug a big pit in their backyard. He filled it with sand. Nancy used this to learn how to hit balls out of sand traps.

When Nancy started to play professional golf, many people complained. They said that she was too focused on her game. They did not like the way she played. The truth was that they did not like to see a Hispanic American woman win so many games. Nancy ignored the prejudice like she always had. She kept working hard. In 1977, she played in six professional events. Her first full year as a professional golfer was 1978. She won nine tournaments. She also won five tournaments in a row. No female golfer has ever beaten her record.

By the time Nancy was 30, she had won 35 tournaments. In 1989, she was added to the Ladies Professional Golf Association (LPGA) Hall of Fame. She was the youngest woman to have that honor.

Nancy set a goal for herself. She wanted to win 50 tournaments before she retired. She almost reached that goal. She retired from full-time play in 2002. She had won 48 times. But, she knew that it was the right time to retire. Her knees were hurt. She had three children. She wanted to spend more time with her family. Nancy left golf, but golfers will never forget the amazing career of Nancy Lopez.

NAME: _____ DATE: _____

NANCY LOPEZ
(1957– _____)

1. This story tells about:

   a. a woman who learned how to play golf.

   b. a girl whose father loved golf.

   c. a woman who overcame prejudice to become a great golfer.

   d. a woman who played golf in the southwestern United States.

2. What does the word **tips** mean in the passage?

   a. money left for a waiter for good service

   b. helpful hints used to improve a skill

   c. the very tops of hills and mountains

   d. the sharp points of needles

3. Number the following events in the order they happened.

   _____ Nancy decided to retire from playing golf full-time to spend time with her family.

   _____ Nancy played in her first six professional events.

   _____ Nancy played on the boys' golf team in high school.

   _____ Nancy won nine tournaments, including five in a row.

   _____ Nancy got her first set of golf clubs.

4. Answer the following questions.

   Where did Nancy Lopez grow up?

   _____

   Who was Nancy's first golf teacher?

   _____

   When did Nancy play her first full year of professional golf?

   _____

   What honor did Nancy receive in 1989?

   _____

5. Why did Nancy's family have to drive 200 miles to play golf?

   a. There were no courses closer to their home.

   b. There were courses closer than that to their home, but they were not good.

   c. They were not allowed to play on nearby courses because they were Hispanic Americans.

   d. They were not allowed to play on nearby courses because Nancy was a girl.

BONUS

Do you think that you would like to play golf? Why or why not? Write a paragraph explaining your feelings.

© Carson-Dellosa • CD-104255 • American Women Achievers

ELLEN OCHOA
(1958– _____)

When Ellen Ochoa was growing up, she did not dream about going into space. At that time, there were no female astronauts in America to act as role models. It was not until Ellen was 20 years old that Sally Ride and five other women were chosen for the space program. By that time, Ellen was in college. More than 10 years later, Ellen was working on her PhD and a group of her friends applied for jobs at the National Aeronautics and Space Administration (NASA). They told Ellen, and she applied, too. It was Ellen who was selected by NASA. She became an astronaut in 1990.

Ellen grew up in La Mesa, California. Her mother loved to learn. She raised five children and went to college at the same time. She could take only one class at a time, so it took Ellen's mother 22 years to finish school. Her mother's hard work made Ellen want to work hard, too.

That was a good thing, because the training at NASA was difficult and demanding. Ellen had to learn how to cope with every kind of emergency that might occur. The hours were long and tiring. Ellen says that being in space was actually much easier than training to go there!

Ellen was the first Hispanic American woman to fly into space. Her first **mission** was in 1993, when she was in space for nine days. It was Ellen's job to launch a satellite, using the shuttle's mechanical arm. She also helped her team conduct research about the atmosphere. She stayed in touch with her family on Earth through e-mail, and on trips that are longer than 10 days, astronauts also get to see their families on video conference calls.

Since that first flight, Ellen has gone into space three more times. She has logged 978 hours in space and worked the mechanical arm on each trip. Ellen loves going into space. She finds it exciting and interesting.

Back on Earth, Ellen has other jobs to do. She worked as an inventor, and one of her inventions helps guide robot systems and make them work more efficiently. Ellen is now in charge of the Astronaut Office at NASA in Houston, Texas. Ellen enjoys going to schools and speaking to students. She wants to demonstrate that they can do anything they want to if they work hard and love learning. That is the same lesson that Ellen's mother taught her.

When Ellen is not working, she spends time with her family. She is married and has two children. She likes to play volleyball and ride her bike. Music is another hobby—Ellen plays the flute. But, her favorite hobby is flying. She pilots a small plane. Even when she cannot go into space, Ellen loves to be in the sky.

ELLEN OCHOA
(1958– _____)

When Ellen Ochoa was growing up, she did not dream about going into space. At that time, there were no female astronauts in America. It was not until Ellen was 20 years old that Sally Ride and five other women were picked for the space program. By that time, Ellen was in college. Ten years later, Ellen was working on her PhD A group of her friends applied for jobs at the National Aeronautics and Space Administration (NASA). They told Ellen. She applied, too. And, Ellen was the person NASA picked. She became an astronaut in 1990.

Ellen grew up in La Mesa, California. Her mother loved to learn. She raised five children and went to college at the same time. She could take only one class at a time. So, it took Ellen's mother 22 years to finish school. Her mother's hard work made Ellen want to work hard, too.

That was a good thing. The training at NASA was hard work. Ellen had to learn how to deal with every kind of event that might go wrong. The hours were long and hard. Ellen says that being in space was much easier than training to go there!

Ellen was the first Hispanic American woman to fly into space. Her first **mission** was in 1993. She was in space for nine days. It was Ellen's job to launch a satellite. She used the shuttle's robot arm to do this. She also helped her team do research about the atmosphere. She stayed in touch with her family on Earth through e-mail. On trips that are longer than 10 days, astronauts also get to see their families on video calls.

Since that first flight, Ellen has gone into space three more times. She has spent 978 hours in space. On each trip, she worked the robot arm. Ellen loves going into space. She finds it exciting and interesting.

Back on Earth, Ellen has other jobs to do. She worked as an inventor. One of her inventions helps guide robot systems and make them work better. Ellen is now in charge of the Astronaut Office at NASA. She works in Houston, Texas. Ellen likes to go to schools and speak to students. She wants to show them that they can do anything they want to if they work hard and love to learn. That is the same lesson that Ellen's mother taught her.

When Ellen is not working, she spends time with her family. She is married and has two children. She likes to play volleyball. She also likes to ride her bike. Music is another hobby. Ellen plays the flute. But, her favorite hobby is flying. She pilots a small plane. Even when she cannot go into space, Ellen loves to be in the sky.

NAME: _____ DATE: _____

ELLEN OCHOA
(1958– _____)

1. The sixth paragraph of this story is mostly about:

   a. how Ellen's mother raised her.

   b. how Ellen trained to go into space.

   c. what jobs Ellen does when she is not in space.

   d. how Ellen feels about space travel.

2. What does the word **mission** mean in the passage?

   a. a group of people sent to a foreign country

   b. a near miss

   c. an outpost built by pioneers or church members

   d. a project in space with special goals

3. Number the following events in the order they happened.

   _____ Ellen grew up in La Mesa, California.

   _____ Ellen was hired by NASA.

   _____ Ellen made three more trips into space.

   _____ Ellen was sent on her first trip into space.

   _____ Ellen worked on her PhD.

4. Answer the following questions.

   Why didn't Ellen dream of going into space as a child?

   _____

   _____

   How many years did it take Ellen's mother to finish college?

   _____

   In what city does Ellen live and work now?

   _____

   What does one of Ellen's inventions do?

   _____

   _____

5. According to the author, why does Ellen like to fly a small plane?

   a. She has flown since she was a young girl.

   b. She likes to be in the sky even when she cannot be in space.

   c. Her mother taught her how to fly.

   d. all of the above

BONUS

What would you like to invent? Draw a picture of your invention. Then, write a description of it.

American Women Achievers • CD-104255 • © Carson-Dellosa

MAYA LIN
(1959– _____)

The **monument** is sometimes called *The Wall*. It is a long, black wall of marble that fans out from a corner. If you look down from above, it looks like an opening book. When you walk to it, you see thousands of names. Each name belongs to someone who died in the Vietnam War.

The person who created the design for this monument is Maya Lin. She was still a student in college when she drew her plans for the design and entered them in a contest in 1981. Maya was thrilled when she won, but she was unprepared for what happened next.

The plan for the black wall of names made some people angry. It was a brand-new idea. Most monuments for wars show soldiers or flags. They make people feel proud and patriotic. But, this wall made visitors look at all of the names of the soldiers who had died, giving people a very different kind of feeling. Some people also complained that Maya is Asian American. They said that she should not make a memorial for a war that was fought in Asia. Other people thought that the wall was ugly. Maya was hurt and scared by all of the anger, criticism, and prejudice.

But then, the monument was built in 1982. Maya's wall was immediately popular. Millions of people came to see it. People touched the names and left flowers and gifts at the wall. They still do.

Maya grew up in Ohio. Both of her parents were teachers at a college; her father was an artist, and her mother taught English. They had left China to start a new life in America. Maya was grown up before her parents would talk to her about their family in China. She found out that her aunt and uncle were famous architects. Maya studied to be an architect in school, too, but she also secretly took art classes.

Today, Maya thinks of herself more as an artist than an architect. She makes monuments that take up large sites. She created an earth sculpture called *Wave Field* for one college. It resembles a Chinese painting, but it is actually a series of little hills and valleys sculpted into the grass.

Another monument that Maya made honors the civil rights movement. It displays the words of Dr. Martin Luther King Jr. He spoke about justice rolling down like water to cover the world. In front of the wall with his quote is a gigantic stone disk. Both the wall and the disk are covered with flowing water.

Today, Maya creates all kinds of things, even furniture. She is shy and stays out of the news, hoping that her strong, beautiful work speaks for itself.

MAYA LIN
(1959– _____)

The **monument** is sometimes called *The Wall*. It is a long, black wall of marble. It fans out from a corner. If you look down from above, it looks like an opening book. When you walk to it, you see thousands of names. Each name belongs to someone who died in the Vietnam War.

The person who had the idea for this monument is Maya Lin. She was still a student in college when she drew her plans for the design. She entered her idea in a contest in 1981. Maya was thrilled when she won. But, she was not ready for what happened next.

The plan for a black wall of names made some people angry. It was a brand-new idea. Most monuments for wars show soldiers or flags. They make people feel proud. But, this wall made visitors look at all of the names of the soldiers who had died. It gave people a very different kind of feeling. Some people also complained that Maya is Asian American. They said that she should not make a monument for a war that was fought in Asia. Other people thought that the wall was ugly. Maya was hurt and scared by all of the anger and prejudice.

But then, the monument was built in 1982. Maya's wall was a big success. Millions of people came to see it. People touched the names. They left flowers and gifts at the wall. They still do.

Maya grew up in Ohio. Both of her parents were teachers at a college. Her father was an artist. Her mother taught English. They had left China. They started a new life in America. Maya was grown up before her parents would talk to her about their family in China. She found out that her aunt and uncle were architects. Maya studied to be an architect in school, too. But, she also secretly took art classes.

Today, Maya thinks of herself more as an artist than an architect. She makes monuments that take up large spaces. She made an earth sculpture called *Wave Field* for one college. It looks like a Chinese painting. But, it is really a series of little hills and valleys built into the grass.

Another monument that Maya made is for the civil rights movement. It shows the words of Dr. Martin Luther King Jr. He spoke about justice rolling down like water to cover the world. In front of the wall with his quote is a big stone disk. Both the wall and the disk are covered with flowing water.

Today, Maya makes all kinds of things, even furniture. She is shy. She stays out of the news. She hopes that her strong, beautiful work speaks for itself.

NAME: _____ DATE: _____

MAYA LIN
(1959– _____)

1. What is the main idea of the third paragraph?

   a. Maya grew up in the United States.

   b. Maya was a good student in college.

   c. Dr. Martin Luther King Jr. liked Maya's idea for the civil rights memorial.

   d. Many people did not like Maya's idea for the Vietnam War monument.

2. What does the word **monument** mean in the passage?

   a. a type of building with more than one floor

   b. something that helps us remember a person or an event

   c. a special place where an architect works

   d. something huge and amazing

3. Number the following events in the order they happened.

   _____ Maya grew up in Ohio.

   _____ Maya entered her idea for a Vietnam War monument in a contest.

   _____ Maya designed a work about the civil rights movement.

   _____ Maya creates designs for furniture.

   _____ Maya's design for the black marble wall was a success.

4. Answer the following questions.

   What did Maya study in college?

   _____

   When did Maya's parents tell her about their family in China?

   _____

   In what year was *The Wall* built?

   _____

   What is *Wave Field*?

   _____
   _____

5. Why did some people say that Maya was the wrong person to design a monument about the Vietnam War?

   a. She is Asian American, and the Vietnam War was fought in Asia.

   b. People were prejudiced against her because of her race.

   c. Some people thought that her design was ugly.

   d. all of the above

BONUS

Have you ever made something that other people did not like? How did you feel? Write about it.

© Carson-Dellosa • CD-104255 • American Women Achievers

SARAH CHANG
(1980– _____)

Sarah Chang says that the violin makes the closest music to the human voice. She has heard that voice all of her life. Sarah was only three years old when she begged her parents for a violin, which she learned how to play right away. Her parents, both musicians, helped her. But, even they were amazed when she got into a famous music school called Juilliard when she was only six years old!

Sarah's father was her first teacher. He also plays the violin. Her mother is a **composer**, a person who writes music. She helped Sarah learn how to read and understand music. Sarah's gift of playing music, though, seems to have been with her all of her life.

Sarah's whole life is dedicated to her gift of music. She started to play with orchestras when she was eight years old. By the time she was nine, she had recorded some of her music for an album. People love to hear her play. One famous musician said that he has never heard a violinist who is closer to being perfect than Sarah.

How does Sarah prepare for her concerts? She practices constantly, playing for four hours a day. She needs to exercise her hands, almost as if she were an athlete. If she does not do that, the muscles in her hands could be strained or weakened.

Sarah has a beautiful violin that was made in Italy in 1717. This violin is so precious that Sarah will not permit it to be photographed. She worries that the hot lights might damage its tone. She also has four different bows, and each one is used for different types of music.

Sarah got a lot of attention when she was a child musician and now thinks that part of her life was relatively easy. Today, she is judged as a grown-up musician, and it is harder for her to get great reviews. But, there are positive things about being older. Now that she is a young adult, Sarah has more control over her life. She gets to pick the pieces she plays and practices. She also chooses the concerts in which she plays.

But, the majority of Sarah's life is planned ahead. She has to travel a lot to play in different destinations. If you ask her where she will be two years from now, she will know what hotel she will be staying in and what she will be practicing on her violin. Sometimes, she does not like that and wishes that she had more free time. But, she says that if she does not touch a violin for three or four days, her fingers start to feel strange. And, she loves to be on the stage, playing music for other people. For her, that is the most significant thing in life.

SARAH CHANG
(1980– _____)

Sarah Chang says that the violin makes the closest music to the human voice. She has heard that voice all of her life. Sarah was only three years old when she begged her parents for a violin. She learned how to play it right away. Her parents, both musicians, helped her. But, they were amazed when she got into a famous music school called Juilliard when she was only six years old!

Sarah's father was her first teacher. He also plays the violin. Her mother is a **composer**, a person who writes music. She helped Sarah learn about reading and understanding music. Sarah's gift of playing music, though, seems to have been with her all of her life.

Sarah's whole life is devoted to her gift of music. She started to play with orchestras when she was eight years old. By the time she was nine, she had recorded some of her music for an album. People love to hear her play. One well-known musician said that he has never heard a violinist who is closer to being perfect than Sarah.

How does Sarah get ready for her concerts? She practices a lot. She plays for four hours a day. She needs to exercise her hands, almost like a sports player. If she does not do that, the muscles in her hands could get strained.

Sarah has a beautiful violin. It was made in Italy in 1717. This violin is very important. Sarah will not let pictures be taken of it. She worries that the hot lights would hurt it. She also has four different bows. Each of them is for different kinds of music.

Sarah got a lot of attention when she was a child musician. She now thinks that that part of her life was easy. Today, she is judged as a grown-up musician. It is harder for her to get great reviews. But, there are good things about being older. Now that she is a young adult, Sarah has more control over her life. She gets to pick the pieces she plays and practices. She chooses the concerts in which she plays.

But, a lot of Sarah's life is planned ahead. She has to travel a lot to play in different places. If you ask her where she will be two years from now, she will know what hotel she will be staying in. And, she will know what she will be practicing on her violin. Sometimes, she does not like that. She wishes that she had more free time. But, she says if she does not touch a violin for three or four days, her fingers start to feel strange. And, she loves to be on the stage, playing music for other people. For her, that is the most important thing in life.

NAME: _____ DATE: _____

SARAH CHANG
(1980– _____)

1. Choose a good title for this story.

   a. How to Play the Violin

   b. A Strange Childhood

   c. A Life of Music

   d. Orchestra Music and Musicians

2. What does the word **composer** mean in the passage?

   a. someone who plays a violin

   b. someone who is very calm

   c. someone who sets type for newspapers

   d. someone who writes music

3. Number the following events in the order they happened.

   _____ Sarah Chang asked her parents for a violin.

   _____ Sarah started going to music school.

   _____ Sarah started playing with orchestras.

   _____ Sarah recorded music for her first CD.

   _____ Sarah gets to choose her own pieces and concerts.

4. Answer the following questions.

   How old was Sarah when she got her first violin?

   _____

   What was the name of the music school that Sarah went to?

   _____

   What jobs do Sarah's parents have?

   _____

   In what year was Sarah's violin made?

   _____

5. Why do you think Sarah's life is planned so far ahead of time?

   a. She has such a busy schedule that orchestras have to plan ahead of time for her to play with them.

   b. She likes to have a lot of time to get ready for each concert.

   c. She does not like to fly in airplanes, so she has to plan slower ways to get to different places in the world.

   d. She needs to spend a lot of time with her parents between concerts.

BONUS

Do you like music? Write a paragraph about your favorite song or your favorite type of music.

ANSWER KEY

Abigail Adams 7
1. c; 2. b; 3. 2, 3, 1, 5, 4;
4. Abigail wanted it to say that women were free, just like men; She thought it was wrong to own slaves; Abigail ran a farm herself, so she was sure that other women could do it; John Quincy Adams was Abigail's son. He became president in 1824; 5. a

Phillis Wheatley 10
1. d; 2. b; 3. 1, 3, 2, 5, 4;
4. She wrote to a friend in London who helped Phillis get the book printed; She did not have to do hard work. She was taught to read and write. She was given time and a place to write; Phillis met Benjamin Franklin in London; Phillis came home because Mrs. Wheatley was ill; 5. d

Sacagawea 13
1. d; 2. c; 3. 2, 4, 5, 1, 3;
4. They were explorers who were working for the U.S. government; The Hidatsa tribe took Sacagawea east; The explorers camped for the winter near the tribe's village; She helped them find the best paths, find food, and talk with other tribes; 5. b

Maria Mitchell 16
1. b; 2. a; 3. 2, 4, 5, 1, 3; 4. The king of Denmark gave Maria a gold medal; Maria took a job at the library so that she could earn money and still read and learn all day; The American Academy of Arts and Sciences made her its first woman member; Maria taught at Vassar College; 5. a

Harriet Tubman 19
1. c; 2. a; 3. 5, 1, 4, 2, 3;
4. Harriet led a group of soldiers on a raid; She used the North Star and the Underground Railroad to find her way to freedom; She was a nurse and a spy during the Civil War; She opened a home for old people. Or, she worked for the rights of women; 5. c

Susan B. Anthony 22
1. a; 2. b; 3. 2, 3, 1, 5, 4; 4. She was a woman who felt the same way about slavery and women's rights as Susan and started a magazine with her; The book was about women's right to vote; Women did not have the right to earn money. Or, to sue. Or, to do certain jobs. Or, to vote; New York passed important new laws for women; 5. c

Emily Dickinson 25
1. b; 2. a; 3. 1, 5, 3, 2, 4;
4. Emily lived in Amherst, Massachusetts; She was so homesick that she came back in less than a year; She rolled them up, locked them in her desk, and sometimes made booklets out of them; Susan was Emily's best friend and sister-in-law; 5. d

Mary Edwards Walker 28
1. a; 2. c; 3. 3, 4, 1, 5, 2; 4. She grew up on a farm in New York; There was one female doctor in the United States before Mary became a doctor; She helped Susan B. Anthony; President Jimmy Carter gave back her Medal of Honor; 5. d

Louisa May Alcott 31
1. a; 2. b; 3. 2, 3, 1, 5, 4;
4. Louisa's father was a teacher; Louisa decided at a young age that she needed to earn money for her family; Jo March is the character like Louisa; She earned money by selling her writing; 5. d

Queen Liliuokalani 34
1. c; 2. c; 3. 5, 3, 4, 2, 1; 4. Her songs were about the people and places of the Hawaiian Islands; Her brother ruled Hawaii before she did; She was kept a prisoner in a room in her palace; She wanted to change the laws that took away her power to help her people; 5. b

Mary Cassatt 37
1. b; 2. d; 3. 3, 2, 5, 1, 4;
4. Edgar Degas was a famous artist and Mary's friend; Paris was the center of the art world at the time; She helped museums buy paintings; She had trouble with her eyes and was almost blind; 5. d

Juliette "Daisy" Gordon Low 40
1. c; 2. a; 3. 5, 2, 4, 3, 1;
4. Daisy had lost most of her hearing; Sir Robert Baden-Powell started the Boy Scouts and the Girl Guides in England; She went to live in England; There were 18 Girl Scouts in the first troop; 5. d

Mary McLeod Bethune 43
1. a; 2. d; 3. 3, 2, 5, 4, 1;
4. Mary started a one-room school, which became Bethune-Cookman College; She had five students in her first class; Mary had 16 brothers and sisters; A white girl took a book away from her, saying, "You can't read that"; 5. c

© Carson-Dellosa • CD-104255 • American Women Achievers

ANSWER KEY

Helen Keller 46
1. d; 2. b; 3. 1, 2, 3, 5, 4;
4. She got very sick and became both blind and deaf; She was Helen's teacher; Helen went to college in 1900; Anne Sullivan taught Helen words by finger-spelling them to her; 5. b

Jeannette Rankin 49
1. d; 2. b; 3. 1, 5, 4, 2, 3;
4. A "Tin Lizzie" is a Model T Ford; Jeannette was born in Montana; She worked for world peace; As a woman, she could not fight in the war, and she refused to send anyone else; 5. d

Eleanor Roosevelt 52
1. a; 2. c; 3. 2, 5, 1, 4, 3;
4. She learned that she was good at many things—she was a good leader, writer, athlete, and friend; She traveled and gave speeches on his behalf; Eleanor's uncle was President Theodore Roosevelt; She became an important part of American politics; 5. b

Mary Pickford 55
1. b; 2. a; 3. 5, 3, 4, 1, 2;
4. Mary Pickford's parents named her Gladys Smith; She acted in a Toronto, Canada, stage play called *The Silver King*; D. W. Griffith was a movie director who hired Mary to make movies; Her movie company was called United Artists; 5. d

Amelia Earhart 58
1. b; 2. d; 3. 5, 1, 4, 2, 3;
4. *Canary* was the name of Amelia's first plane; Fred Noonan was the navigator she chose for her flight around the world; Amelia went on her first flight in 1920; She was making a trip around the world; 5. b

Margaret Bourke-White 61
1. d; 2. c; 3. 3, 2, 5, 4, 1;
4. She helped her father develop pictures when she was little; He was a writer with whom Margaret worked; She liked to take pictures of working people, factories, mills, and plants; She took pictures in the South in the 1930s; 5. a

Rachel Carson 64
1. c; 2. c; 3. 1, 3, 5, 2, 4;
4. She felt that it was more important to write about the dangers of DDT in the short time she had left to live; President John F. Kennedy put together a group to study the problem she had discovered; She studied wildlife and the biology of the sea; The article talks about four of her books; 5. d

Virginia Apgar 67
1. d; 2. c; 3. 2, 1, 4, 5, 3; 4. It is a scale to judge whether a baby needs help during the first few minutes after birth; Columbia University hired Virginia; She grew up in New Jersey; Virginia's hobbies included fishing, watching baseball games, playing the violin, and making violins; 5. b

Babe Didrikson Zaharias 70
1. c; 2. a; 3. 3, 4, 5, 2, 1;
4. Babe's first sport was basketball; Babe's husband, wrestler George Zaharias, became her manager; She helped start a professional tour for female golfers; She won three Olympic medals—two gold and one silver; 5. d

Rosa Parks 73
1. c; 2. a; 3. 2, 5, 4, 3, 1;
4. Rosa would not give her seat on the bus to a white man when he told her to; She lived in Montgomery, Alabama; Rosa sewed clothing; The Supreme Court ruled that the bus laws were wrong; 5. a

Eunice Shriver 76
1. b; 2. c; 3. 3, 2, 5, 4, 1;
4. She was Eunice's sister; Eunice wanted other children like Rosemary to have a chance to play outdoor games; The first Special Olympics were held in Chicago, Illinois; She started an organization to help the athletes train, raised money, and found volunteers; 5. d

Maria Tallchief 79
1. c; 2. b; 3. 1, 3, 4, 5, 2; 4. Her family got the money from oil found on the land of the Osage Nation; He married Maria and created dances for her; They started their dance group in Chicago; She danced the part of the Sugar Plum Fairy in *The Nutcracker*; 5. d

Althea Gibson 82
1. c; 2. c; 3. 1, 4, 3, 2, 5;
4. The first sport she played was paddle tennis; She wrote an essay asking that Althea be allowed to play in major tennis events; Althea grew up in Harlem, New York; Althea became a tennis teacher; 5. a

ANSWER KEY

Sandra Day O'Connor 85

1. c; 2. a; 3. 2, 4, 5, 1, 3; 4. The Supreme Court is the highest court in the U.S.; The Lazy-B was a ranch in Texas where Sandra was raised; She was a justice of the Supreme Court for 25 years; President Ronald Reagan asked her to serve on the court; 5. b

Toni Morrison 88

1. b; 2. b; 3. 3, 2, 4, 5, 1; 4. She grew up in Ohio; Her father told her stories and folktales; *Beloved* came out in 1987; Her son, Slade, helps her write them; 5. d

Rita Moreno 91

1. a; 2. d; 3. 2, 3, 4, 1, 5; 4. She won the Oscar®, the Emmy®, the Tony®, and the Grammy®; They came from Puerto Rico; She acted in *The Electric Company* and *The Muppet Show*; She got small, boring parts playing Hispanic women, American Indians, and a slave princess in Thailand; 5. d

Madeleine Albright...........94

1. a; 2. c; 3. 4, 5, 1, 2, 3; 4. They came to the United States to escape the Russian army that took over their homeland; President Bill Clinton asked Congress to make her secretary of state; She works for the Council of Women World Leaders; She learned Russian when she was in the hospital after she had twins; 5. a

Pat Mora 97

1. a; 2. c; 3. 2, 4, 1, 3, 5; 4. She feels that poets are healers who build bridges between people; It took her eight years; The character in her tall tale is Doña Flor; She grew up in El Paso, Texas, near the border between Texas and Mexico; 5. d

Isabel Allende................ 100

1. a; 2. d; 3. 2, 4, 3, 5, 1; 4. She worked for the United Nations; She started writing a letter to her grandfather; She became an American citizen in 2003; They left Chile because they were in danger; 5. a

Antonia Novello 103

1. b; 2. b; 3. 1, 5, 4, 2, 3; 4. Her home was in Puerto Rico; Her mother made sure that Antonia had the best teachers; She became the surgeon general in 1990; She helped them get information about illnesses when they were writing laws; 5. d

Sue Hendrickson............ 106

1. b; 2. a; 3. 1, 3, 4, 2, 5; 4. She learned how to dive so that she could collect tropical fish and sell them to pet stores; She went to the desert of Peru; She discovered the *T. rex* skeleton in 1990; It was sunk in a battle; 5. c

Sally Ride 109

1. b; 2. c; 3. 5, 3, 4, 1, 2; 4. She quit college to become a professional tennis player; Eight thousand people asked for places in the program; Sally first went into space in 1983; She helps them learn more about science and math through the Sally Ride Science Club, through her NASA program that lets them take photos of Earth from space, and through writing children's books; 5. d

Oprah Winfrey............... 112

1. b; 2. d; 3. 2, 5, 4, 1, 3; 4. She was not a good news reporter because she let her emotions show too much; She lived in Nashville, Tennessee, with her father; Her TV show began showing around the country in 1986; She started a school for girls there; 5. a

Nancy Lopez.................. 115

1. c; 2. b; 3. 5, 3, 2, 4, 1; 4. She grew up in New Mexico; Nancy's father was her first golf teacher; She played her first full year of professional golf in 1978; She was added to the LPGA Hall of Fame in 1989; 5. c

Ellen Ochoa................... 118

1. c; 2. d; 3. 1, 3, 5, 4, 2; 4. There were no female astronauts in America at that time to act as role models; It took Ellen's mother 22 years to finish college; She now lives and works in Houston, Texas; One of her inventions helps guide robot systems and make them work better; 5. b

Maya Lin 121

1. d; 2. b; 3. 1, 2, 4, 5, 3; 4. Maya studied architecture and art in college; They told Maya about their family in China when she was grown up; *The Wall* was built in 1982; *Wave Field* is an earth sculpture that Maya Lin designed and built; 5. d

Sarah Chang 124

1. c; 2. d; 3. 1, 2, 3, 4, 5; 4. Sarah was three years old when she got her first violin; The name of the music school was Juilliard; Sarah's father plays the violin. Her mother is a composer; Sarah's violin was made in 1717; 5. a

ASSESSMENT GRID

	MAIN IDEA (Question 1)	CONTEXT CLUES (Question 2)	SEQUENTIAL ORDER (Question 3)	READING FOR DETAILS (Question 4)	DRAWING CONCLUSIONS (Question 5)
Abigail Adams					
Phillis Wheatley					
Sacagawea					
Maria Mitchell					
Harriet Tubman					
Susan B. Anthony					
Emily Dickinson					
Mary Edwards Walker					
Louisa May Alcott					
Queen Liliuokalani					
Mary Cassatt					
Juliette "Daisy" Gordon Low					
Mary McLeod Bethune					
Helen Keller					
Jeannette Rankin					
Eleanor Roosevelt					
Mary Pickford					
Amelia Earhart					
Margaret Bourke-White					
Rachel Carson					
Virginia Apgar					
Babe Didrikson Zaharias					
Rosa Parks					
Eunice Shriver					
Maria Tallchief					
Althea Gibson					
Sandra Day O'Connor					
Toni Morrison					
Rita Moreno					
Madeleine Albright					
Pat Mora					
Isabel Allende					
Antonia Novello					
Sue Hendrickson					
Sally Ride					
Oprah Winfrey					
Nancy Lopez					
Ellen Ochoa					
Maya Lin					
Sarah Chang					